INDIANS

INDIANS

A PLAY BY

 Arthur Kopit

A SPOTLIGHT DRAMABOOK

HILL & WANG New York

A division of Farrar, Straus and Giroux

COPYRIGHT © 1969 BY ARTHUR KOPIT
ALL RIGHTS RESERVED
STANDARD BOOK NUMBER (CLOTH EDITION): 8090–5756–5
STANDARD BOOK NUMBER (PAPERBACK EDITION): 8090–1218–9
LIBRARY OF CONGRESS CATALOG CARD NUMBER: 69–16835
MANUFACTURED IN THE UNITED STATES OF AMERICA
FIRST EDITION OCTOBER 1969

Fourteenth printing, 1983

The halftone illustrations in this volume are from the New York production of Indians. *Photographs are by Martha Swope. The poster reproduced on pages 58 and 59 is by courtesy of the New York Public Library, the Theater Collection.*

For Leslie

Acknowledgments

The idea for this play occurred to me in March, 1966. Since then, there have been many persons whose help has been instrumental in the play's reaching its final form: first, my producer, Lyn Austin, to whom I described its basic concept, and who gave me an advance of money so I could afford to research the necessary historical material; then, the wonderful actors and staff of the Royal Shakespeare Company, who presented the play some two years later, and especially Jack Gelber, who directed the excellent London production, and whose firsthand knowledge of the American Indians was constantly invaluable; Zelda Fitchandler and the staff and actors of the Arena Stage, where the next and greatly rewritten version of the play was produced, which afforded me still another relatively unstressful opportunity to view what I had written; Gene Frankel, who staged the Washington and New York productions and asked a seemingly endless number of incisive, important, and fundamental questions; my agent, Audrey Wood, who—with great affection—kept urging further rewrites, and who only smiled when I said I thought this enterprise threatened to become a lifelong task. I would particularly like to thank the Rockefeller Foundation, which gave me a grant of money so my wife and I could live in Europe during the time my play was in production there, and then allowed us to go, immediately after the production, to the fantastic Villa Serbelloni, at Lake Como, where the basic rethinking and fundamental reshaping of the play was done.

Indians was first performed by the Royal Shakespeare Company on July 4, 1968, at the Aldwych Theatre, London. Its American première was on May 6, 1969, at the Arena Stage, Washington, D. C.

Characters

Indians opened in New York at the Brooks Atkinson Theatre on October 13, 1969, with the following cast:

BUFFALO BILL   Stacy Keach
SITTING BULL   Manu Tupou
SENATOR LOGAN   Tom Aldredge
SENATOR DAWES   Richard McKenzie
SENATOR MORGAN   Jon Richards
TRIAL SOLDIERS   Bob Hamilton, Richard Nieves
JOHN GRASS   Sam Waterston
SPOTTED TAIL   James J. Sloyan
GRAND DUKE ALEXIS   Raul Julia
INTERPRETER   Yusef Bulos
NED BUNTLINE   Charles Durning
GERONIMO   Ed Rombola
MASTER VALET   Darryl Croxton
FIRST LADY   Dortha Duckworth
OL' TIME PRESIDENT   Peter MacLean
WILD BILL HICKOK   Barton Heyman
TESKANJAVILA   Dimitra Arliss
UNCAS   Raul Julia
WHITE HOUSE ORCHESTRA   Tony Posk, Peter Rosenfelt
VALETS   Joseph Ragno, Richard Novello, Brian Donohue
CHIEF JOSEPH   George Mitchell

ANNIE OAKLEY   Pamela Grey
JESSE JAMES   Ronny Cox
BILLY THE KID   Ed Rombola
PONCHO   Raul Julia
BARTENDER   Brian Donohue
COWBOYS   Richard Nieves, Richard Miller, Clint Allmon, Bob
 Hamilton
COLONEL FORSYTH   Peter MacLean
LIEUTENANT   Richard Novello
REPORTERS   Ronny Cox, Brian Donohue, Darryl Croxton
CRAZY HORSE   Dino Laudicina
HE-WHO-HEARS-THUNDER   Robert McLean
RED CLOUD   Andy Torres
LITTLE HAWK   Jay Fletcher
KIOKUK   Princeton Dean
SATANTA   Ed Henkel
OLD TAZA   Michael Ebbin
BLACK HAWK   Kevin Conway
TECUMSEH   Pascual Vaquer
YELLOW CLOUD   Wesley Fata
KICKING BEAR   Gary Weber
TOUCH-THE-CLOUDS   Peter DeMaio
HOWLING WOLF   Ted Goodridge
WHITE ANTELOPE   Tom Fletcher
LOW DOG   Philip Arsenault
NAICHE   Juan Antonio
INDIAN DRUMMERS   Leon Oxman, Allan Silverman

Director, Gene Frankel; Setting, Oliver Smith; Lighting, Thomas
Skelton; Costumes, Marjorie Slaiman; Music, Richard Peaslee;
Choreography, Julie Arenal; Associate Producer, Steven Sinn;
Production Assistant, Binti Hoskins

xii

Chronology for a Dreamer

1846 William F. Cody born in Le Claire, Iowa, on February 26.

1866 Geronimo surrenders.

1868 William Cody accepts employment to provide food for railroad workers; kills 4,280 buffaloes. Receives nickname "Buffalo Bill."

1869 *Buffalo Bill, the King of the Border Men,* a dime novel by Ned Buntline, makes Buffalo Bill a national hero.

1872 Expedition west in honor of Grand Duke Alexis of Russia, Buffalo Bill as guide.

1876 Battle at the Little Big Horn; Custer killed.

1877 Chief Joseph surrenders.

1878 Buffalo Bill plays himself in *Scouts of the Plains,* a play by Ned Buntline.

1879 Wild Bill Hickok joins Buffalo Bill on the stage.

1883 Sitting Bull surrenders, is sent to Standing Rock Reservation.

1883 "Buffalo Bill's Wild West Show" gives first performance, is great success.

1885 Sitting Bull allowed to join Wild West Show, tours with company for a year.

1886   United States Commission visits Standing Rock Reservation to investigate Indian grievances.

1890   Sitting Bull assassinated, December 15.

1890   Wounded Knee Massacre, December 25.

The play derives, in part, from this chronology but does not strictly adhere to it.—A.K.

Scene 1

(Audience enters to stage with no curtain. House lights dim.
On stage: three large glass cases, one holding a larger-than-life-size effigy of Buffalo Bill in fancy embroidered buckskin. One, an effigy of Sitting Bull dressed in simple buckskin or cloth, no headdress, little if any ornamentation. The last case contains some artifacts: a buffalo skull, a bloodstained Indian shirt, and an old rifle. The surrounding stage is dark. The cases are lit by spotlights from above.
Strange music coming from all about. Sense of dislocation.
The house lights fade to dark.
Music up.
Lights on the cases slowly dim.
Sound of wind, soft at first.
The cases glide into the shadowy distance and disappear.
Eerie light now on stage; dim spotlights sweep the floor as if trying to locate something in space.
Brief, distorted strains of Western American music.
A VOICE *reverberates from all about the theatre.*
    VOICE
Cody . . . *Cody* . . . *Cody!* . . . *CODY!*
(One of the spotlights passes something: a man on a horse. The spotlight slowly retraces itself, picks up the horse and rider. They are in a far corner of the stage; they move in slow motion.

The other spotlights now move toward them, until all converge. At first, the light is dim. As they come toward us, it gets brighter.

The man is BUFFALO BILL, *dressed as in the museum case. The horse is a glorious white artificial stallion with wild, glowing eyes.*

They approach slowly, their slow motion gradually becoming normal speed.

Vague sound of cheering heard. Music becoming rodeolike. More identifiable.

Then, slowly, from the floor, an open-framed oval fence rises and encloses them.

The horse shies.

Tiny lights, strung beneath the top bar of the fence, glitter faintly. The spotlights—multicolored—begin to crisscross about the oval.

Ghostly-pale Wild West Show banners slowly descend.

Then! It's a WILD WEST SHOW!

Loud, brassy music!

Lights blazing everywhere!

The horse rears. His rider whispers a few words, calms him.

Then, a great smile on his face, BUFFALO BILL *begins to tour the ring, one hand lightly gripping the reins, the other proudly waving his big Stetson to the unseen surrounding crowd. Surely it is a great sight; the horse prances, struts, canters, dances to the music, leaps softly through the light,* BUFFALO BILL *effortlessly in control of the whole world, the universe; eternity.)*

BUFFALO BILL

Yessir, BACK AGAIN! That triumphant brassy music, those familiar savage drums! Should o' known I couldn't stay away! Should o' known here's where I belong! The heat o' that ol' spotlight on my face. Yessir. . . . Should o' known here's where I belong. . . .

The set model

(*He takes a deep breath, closes his eyes, savors the air. A pause.*)
Reminded o' somethin' tol' me once by General Custer. You remember him—one o' the great dumbass men in history. Not fer nothin' that he graduated last in his class at West Point! Anyways, we was out on the plains one day, when he turned t' me, with a kind o' far-off look in his eye, an' said, "Bill! If there is one thing a man must never fear, it's makin' a personal comeback."
(*He chuckles.*)
Naturally, I——

    VOICE
(*Softly.*)
And now, to start . . .

    BUFFALO BILL
(*Startled.*)
Hm?

    VOICE
And now to start.

    BUFFALO BILL
But I . . . just . . . got up here.

    VOICE
I'm sorry; it's time to start.

    BUFFALO BILL
Can't you *wait a second?* WHAT'S THE RUSH? *WAIT A SECOND!*
(*Silence. He takes a deep breath; quiets his horse down.*)
I'm sorry. But if I seem a trifle edgy to you, it's only 'cause I've just come from a truly harrowing engagement; seems my . . . manager, a . . . rather *ancient* gentleman, made a terrible *mistake* an' booked me int' what turned out t' be a ghost town! Well! I dunno what you folks know 'bout show business, but le' me tell you, there is nothin' more depressin' than playin' two-a-day in a goddam ghost town!
(*He chuckles.*

INDIANS *appear around the outside of the ring.*

The horse senses their presence and shies; BUFFALO BILL, *as if realizing what it means, turns in terror.*)

VOICE

Bill.

BUFFALO BILL

But——

VOICE

It's *time.*

(*Pause.*)

BUFFALO BILL

Be—before we start, I'd . . . just like to say——

VOICE

Bill!

(*The* INDIANS *slowly approach.*)

BUFFALO BILL

——*to say* that . . . I am a fine man. And anyone who says otherwise is *WRONG!*

VOICE

(*Softly.*)

Bill, *it's time.*

BUFFALO BILL

My life is an open book; I'm not *ashamed* of its bein' looked at!

VOICE

(*Coaxing tone.*)

Bill . . .

BUFFALO BILL

I'm sorry, this is very . . . hard . . . for me t' say. But I believe I . . . am a . . . hero. . . . *A GODDAM HERO!*

(*Indian music.*

His horse rears wildly.

Lights change for next scene.)

BUFFALO BILL (Stacy Keach)

Scene 2

(*Light up on* SITTING BULL. *He is dressed simply—no feathered headdress. It is winter.*)

SITTING BULL

I am Sitting Bull! . . . In the moon of the first snow-falling, in the year half my people died from hunger, the Great Father sent three wise men . . . to investigate the conditions of our reservation, though we'd been promised he would come himself.

(*Lights up on* SENATORS LOGAN, MORGAN, *and* DAWES; *they are flanked by armed* SOLDIERS. *Opposite them, in a semicircle, are* SITTING BULL's *people, all huddling in tattered blankets from the cold.*)

SENATOR LOGAN

Indians! Please be assured that this committee has not come to punish you or take away any of your land but only to hear your grievances, determine if they are just. And if so, remedy them. For we, like the Great Father, wish only the best for our Indian children.

(*The* SENATORS *spread out various legal documents.*)

SITTING BULL

They were accompanied by . . . my friend, William Cody——
(*Enter* BUFFALO BILL, *collar of his overcoat turned up for the wind.*)

in whose Wild West Show I'd once appeared . . .

(BUFFALO BILL *greets a number of the* INDIANS.)

in exchange for some food, a little clothing. And a beautiful horse that could do tricks.

SENATOR MORGAN

Colonel Cody has asked if he might say a few words before testimony begins.

SENATOR LOGAN

We would be honored.

BUFFALO BILL

(*To the* INDIANS.)

My . . . brothers.

(*Pause.*)

I know how disappointed you all must be that the Great Father isn't here; I apologize for having said I thought I . . . could bring him.

(*Pause.*)

However! The three men I *have* brought are by far his most trusted personal representatives. And I promise that talking to them will be the same as . . .

(*Pause. Softly.*)

. . . talking to him.

(*Long pause; he rubs his eyes as if to soothe a headache.*)

To . . . Sitting Bull, then . . .

(*He stares at* SITTING BULL.)

. . . I would like to say that I hope you can overlook your . . . disappointment. And remember what is at *stake* here. And not get angry . . . or too impatient.

(*Pause.*)

Also, I hope you will ask your people to speak with open hearts when talking to these men. And treat them with the same great respect I have always . . . shown . . . to you, for these men have come to *help* you and your people. And I am afraid they may be the only ones left, now, who can.

SITTING BULL

And though there were many among us who wanted to speak first: men like Red Cloud! And Little Hawk! And He-Who-Hears-Thunder! And Crazy Horse! Men who were great war-

riors, and had counted many coups! And been with us at the
Little Big Horn when we *KILLED CUSTER!* . . .

(*Pause.*)

I would not let them speak. . . . For they were like me, and
tended to get angry, easily.

(*Pause.*)

Instead, I asked the *young* man, John Grass, who had never
fought at all, but had been to the white man's school at Carlisle.
And *thought* he understood . . . something . . . of their ways.

BUFFALO BILL

Sitting Bull would like John Grass to speak first.

LOGAN

Call John Grass.

BUFFALO BILL

John Grass! Come forward.

(*Enter* JOHN GRASS *in a black cutaway many sizes too small for
him. He wears an Indian shirt. Around his neck is a medal.*)

JOHN GRASS

Brothers! I am going to talk about what the Great Father told
us a long time ago. He told us to give up hunting and start
farming. So we did as he said, and our people grew hungry. For
the land was suited to grazing not farming, and even if we'd
been farmers, nothing could have grown. So the Great Father
said he would send us food and clothing, but nothing came of
it. So we asked him for the money he had promised us when
we sold him the Black Hills, thinking, with this money we
could *buy* food and clothing. But nothing came of it. So we
grew ill and sad. . . . So to help us from this sadness, he sent
Bishop Marty, to teach us to be Christians. But when we told
him we did not wish to be Christians but wished to be like our
fathers, and dance the sundance, and fight bravely against
the Shawnee and the Crow! And pray to the Great Spirits who
made the four winds, and the earth, and made man from the
dust of this earth, Bishop Marty hit us! . . . So we said to the
Great Father that we thought we would like to go *back* to
hunting, because to live, we needed food. But we found that

9

while we had been learning to farm, the buffalo had gone away. And the plains were filled now only with their bones. . . . Before we give you any more of our land, or move from here where the people we loved are growing white in their coffins, we want you to tell the Great Father to give us, who still live, what he promised he would! *No more than that.*

SITTING BULL

I prayed for the return of the buffalo!

(*Lights fade to black on everyone but* BUFFALO BILL.

Distant gunshot heard offstage.

Pause.

Two more gunshots.

Lights to black on BUFFALO BILL.)

Scene 3

(*Light up on* SPOTTED TAIL, *standing on a ledge above the plains.*

It is night, and he is lit by a pale moon.

The air is hot. No wind.

A rifle shot is heard offstage, of much greater presence than the previous shots.

SPOTTED TAIL *peers in its direction.*

Sound, offstage, of wounded bulls.

Enter an INDIAN *dressed as a buffalo, wounded in the eye and bellowing with pain.*

He circles the stage.

Enter two more buffaloes, also wounded in the eyes.

The first buffalo dies.

The two other buffaloes stagger over to his side and die beside him; another buffalo [missing an eye] enters, staggers in a circle, senses the location of the dead buffaloes and heads dizzily toward them—dying en route, halfway there.

SPOTTED TAIL *crouches and gazes down at them. Then he stares up at the sky.*

Night creatures screech in the dark.

A pause.)

    BUFFALO BILL

(*Offstage but coming closer.*)

Ninety-three, ninety-four, ninety-five . . . ninety-*six!* I *DID IT!*

(*Enter, running, a much younger* BUFFALO BILL, *rifle in hand, followed shortly by* MEMBERS OF THE U. S. CAVALRY *bearing torches, and the* GRAND DUKE'S INTERPRETER.)

I did it, I did it! No one believed I could, but *I did it!* One hundred buffalo—one hundred shots! "You jus' gimme some torches," I said. "I *know* there's buffalo around us. *Here.* Put yer ear t' the ground. Feel it tremblin'? Well. You wanna see somethin' fantastic, you get me some torches. I'll shoot the reflections in their eyes. I'll shoot 'em like they was so many shiny nickels!"

INTERPRETER

I'll tell the Grand Duke you did what you said. I know he'll be pleased.

BUFFALO BILL

Well he oughta be! I don' give exhibitions like this fer just anybody!

(*Exit the* INTERPRETER.)

'Specially as these critters're gettin' so damn hard t' find.

(*To the* SOLDIERS.)

Not like the ol' days when I was huntin' 'em fer the railroads. (*He laughs, gazes down at one of the buffaloes. Pause. He looks away; squints as if in pain.*)

A SOLDIER

Are you all right, sir?

BUFFALO BILL

Uh . . . yes. Fine.

(*Exit the* SOLDIERS.

BUFFALO BILL *rubs his head.*

SPOTTED TAIL *hops down from his perch and walks up behind* CODY *unnoticed; stares at him.*

Pause.

BUFFALO BILL *senses the Indian's presence and turns, cocking his rifle. The Indian makes no move.*

BUFFALO BILL *stares at the Indian.*

Pause.)

BUFFALO BILL
Spotted Tail! My God. I haven't seen you in years. How . . . ya been?
(*Slight laugh.*)

SPOTTED TAIL
What are you doing here?
(*Pause.*)

BUFFALO BILL
Well, well, what . . . are *you* doing here? This isn't Sioux territory!

SPOTTED TAIL
It isn't *your* territory either.
(*Pause.*)

BUFFALO BILL
Well I'm with . . . these *people.* I'm scoutin' for 'em.

SPOTTED TAIL
These people . . . must be very hungry.

BUFFALO BILL
Hm?

SPOTTED TAIL
To need so many buffalo.

BUFFALO BILL
Ah! Of course! You were following the buffalo *also!* . . . Well listen, I'm sure my friends won't mind you takin' some. 'Tween us, my friends don't 'specially care for the *taste* o' buffalo meat.
(*He laughs.*)
My God, but it's good t' see you again!

SPOTTED TAIL
Your friends: I have been studying them from the hills. They are very strange. They seem neither men, nor women.

BUFFALO BILL

Well! Actually, they're sort of a new *breed* o' people. Called dudes.

(*He chuckles.*)

SPOTTED TAIL

You *like* them?

BUFFALO BILL

Well . . . sure. Why not?

(*Pause.*)

I mean, obviously, they ain't the sort I've been used to. But then, things're changin' out here. An' these men are the ones who're changin' 'em. So, if you wanna be *part* o' these things, an' not left behind somewhere, you jus' plain hafta get *used* to 'em. You—uh—follow . . . what I mean?

(*Silence.*)

I mean . . . you've got to *adjust*. To the times. Make a *plan* fer yerself. I have one. You should have one, too. Fer yer own good. Believe me.

(*Long pause.*)

SPOTTED TAIL

What is your plan?

BUFFALO BILL

Well, my plan is t' help people. Like you, ferinstance. Or these people I'm with. More . . . even . . . than that, maybe. And, and, whatever . . . it is I *do* t' help, for it, these people may someday jus' possibly name streets after me. Cities. Counties. States! I'll . . . be as famous as Dan'l Boone! . . . An' somewhere, on top of a beautiful mountain that overlooks more plains 'n rivers than any other mountain, there might even be a statue of me sittin' on a great white horse, a-wavin' my hat t' everyone down below, thankin' 'em, fer thankin' me, fer havin' done . . . whatever . . . it is I'm gonna . . . *do* fer 'em all. How . . . come you got such a weird look on yer face?

BUNTLINE

(*Offstage.*)

HEY, CODY! *STAY WHERE YA ARE!*

BUFFALO BILL

DON' WORRY! I AIN'T BUDGIN'!

(*To* SPOTTED TAIL.)

That's Mister Ned Buntline, the well-known newspaper reporter. I think he's gonna do an *article* on me! General Custer, who's in charge, an' I think is pushin' fer an article on *himself*, says this may well be the most important western expedition since Lewis 'n Clark.

BUNTLINE

(*Offstage.*)

BY THE WAY, *WHERE* ARE YA?

BUFFALO BILL

I . . . AIN'T SURE! JUST HEAD FOR THE LIGHTS!

(*He laughs to himself.*)

SPOTTED TAIL

Tell me. Who is the man everyone always bows to?

BUFFALO BILL

Oh! The Gran' Duke! He's from a place called Russia. This whole shindig's in his honor. I'm sure he'd love t' meet you. He's never seen a real Indian.

SPOTTED TAIL

There are no Indians in Russia?

(BUFFALO BILL *shakes his head.*)

Then I will study him even more carefully than the others. Maybe if he takes me back to Russia with him, I will not end like my people will . . . end.

BUFFALO BILL

(*Startled.*)

What?

SPOTTED TAIL

I mean, like these fools here, on the ground.

(*He stares at the buffalo.*)

BUFFALO BILL

Ah . . . Well, if ya don' mind my sayin', I think you're bein' a bit pessimistic. But you do what ya like. Jus' remember: these people you're studyin'—some folk think *they're* the fools.

SPOTTED TAIL

Oh, no! They are not fools! *No one who is a white man can be a fool.*
(*He smiles coldly at Buffalo Bill; heraldic Russian fanfare off-stage.*

Enter RUSSIAN TORCHBEARERS *and* TRUMPETEERS.

BUFFALO BILL *and* SPOTTED TAIL, *in awe, back away.*

Enter with much pomp and ceremony GRAND DUKE ALEXIS *on a splendid litter carved like a horse. He is accompanied by his* INTERPRETER, *who points out the four buffaloes to the* GRAND DUKE *as he majestically circles the clearing. He is followed by* NED BUNTLINE, *who carries a camera and tripod.*)

BUFFALO BILL

My God, but that is a beautiful sight!
(*The* GRAND DUKE *comes to a halt. Majestic sweep of his arms to those around him.*)

GRAND DUKE

(*Makes a regal Russian speech.*)

INTERPRETER

His Excellency the Grand Duke wishes to express his heart-felt admiration of Buffalo Bill . . .
(*Music up.*)
. . . for having done what he has done tonight.
(*The* GRAND DUKE *gestures majestically. The* INTERPRETER *opens a small velvet box. Airy music. The* INTERPRETER *walks toward* BUFFALO BILL.)

GRAND DUKE

(*Gesturing for* BUFFALO BILL *to come forward.*)
Boofilo Beel!
(BUFFALO BILL *walks solemnly forward. The* INTERPRETER *takes out a medal.* BUFFALO BILL, *deeply moved, looks around, embarrassed.*

The INTERPRETER *smiles and holds up the medal, gestures warmly for* BUFFALO BILL *to kneel. He does so.*

The INTERPRETER *places the medal, which is on a bright ribbon, around his neck.*

Flashgun goes off.)
BUNTLINE
Great picture, Cody! FRONT PAGE! My God, what a night!
What a story! Uh . . . sorry, yer Highness. Didn't mean t'
distoib ya.
(*He backs meekly away. Sets up his camera for another shot.
The* GRAND DUKE *regains his composure.*)
GRAND DUKE
(*Russian speech.*)
INTERPRETER
His Excellency wonders how Buffalo Bill became such a deadly
shot.
BUFFALO BILL
Oh, well, you know, just . . . practice.
(*Embarrassed laugh.*)
GRAND DUKE
(*Russian speech.*)
INTERPRETER
His Excellency says he wishes that his stupid army knew how
to practice.
GRAND DUKE
(*Russian speech.*)
INTERPRETER
Better yet, he wishes you would come back with him to his
palace and protect him yourself.
BUFFALO BILL
Oh.
(*Slight laugh.*)
Well, I'm sure the Grand Duke's in excellent hands.
(*The* INTERPRETER *whispers what* BUFFALO BILL *has just said.*)
GRAND DUKE
Da! *Hands.*
(*He holds out his hands, then turns them and puts them around
his throat.*)
BUFFALO BILL
I think His Majesty's exaggeratin'. I can't believe he's not *sur-
rounded* by friends.

GRAND DUKE

FRIENDS!

(*He cackles and draws his sword, slashes the air.*)

Friends! Friends! . . . *Friends!*

(*He fights them off.*)

BUFFALO BILL

(*To* BUNTLINE.)

I think he's worried 'bout somethin'.

BUNTLINE

Very strange behavior.

GRAND DUKE

(*Nervous Russian speech.*)

INTERPRETER

His Excellency wonders if Buffalo Bill has ever been afraid.

BUFFALO BILL

. . . Afraid?

GRAND DUKE

(*Russian word.*)

INTERPRETER

Outnumbered.

BUFFALO BILL

Ah.

(*Slight laugh.*)

Well, uh——

BUNTLINE

Go on, tell 'm. It'll help what I'm plannin' t' write.

BUFFALO BILL

(*Delighted.*)

It *will?*

BUNTLINE

Absolutely. Look: de West is changin'—right? Well, people wanna know about it. Wanna feel . . . *part* o' things. I think *you're* what dey need. Someone t' listen to, observe, *identify* wid. No, no, really! I been studyin' you.

BUFFALO BILL

. . . You have?

BUNTLINE

I think you could be de inspiration o' dis land.

BUFFALO BILL

Now I *know* you're foolin'!

BUNTLINE

Not at all. . . . Well go on. Tell 'm what he wants t' hear. T'rough my magic pen, others will hear also. . . . Donmentionit. De nation needs men like me, too.

(*He pats* CODY *on the shoulder and shoves him off toward the* GRAND DUKE; CODY *gathers his courage.*)

BUFFALO BILL

(*To the* GRAND DUKE.)

Well, uh . . . where can I begin? Certainly it's true that I've been outnumbered. And—uh—many times. Yes.

BUNTLINE

That's the way.

BUFFALO BILL

More times, in fact, than I can count.

BUNTLINE

Terrific.

BUFFALO BILL

(*Warming to the occasion.*)

An' believe me, I can count pretty high!

BUNTLINE

SENSATIONAL!

BUFFALO BILL

Mind you, 'gainst *me*, twelve's normally an even battle—long's I got my two six-shooters that is.

BUNTLINE

Keep it up, keep it up!

BUFFALO BILL

THIRTEEN! If one of 'em's thin enough for a bullet t' go clean through. Fourteen if I got a huntin' knife. Fifteen if there's a hard surface off o' which I can ricochet a few shots.

BUNTLINE

Go on!

BUFFALO BILL

Um, twenty . . . if I got a stick o' dynamite. HUNDRED! IF THERE'S ROCKS T' START A AVALANCHE!

(BUNTLINE *applauds.*)

What I mean is, with *me* it's never say die! Why . . . I remember once I was ridin' for the Pony Express 'tween Laramie 'n Tombstone. Suddenly, jus' past the Pecos, fifty drunk Comanches attack. Noise like a barroom whoop-di-do, arrows fallin' like hailstones! I mean, they come on me so fast they don' have time t' see my face, notice who I am, realize I'm in fact a very good *friend* o' theirs!

GRAND DUKE

FRIEND! FRIEND!

BUNTLINE

(*Sotto voce.*)

Get off de subject!

BUFFALO BILL

Well, there was no alternative but t' fire back. Well I'd knocked off 'bout thirty o' their number when I realized I was *out* o' bullets. Just at that moment, a arrow whizzed past my head. Thinkin' fast, I reached out an' caught it. Then, usin' it like a fly swatter, I knocked away the other nineteen arrows that were headin' fer my heart. Whereupon, I stood up in the stirrups, hurled the arrow sixty yards. . . . An' killed their chief.

(*Pause.*)

Which . . . *depressed* . . . the remainin' Indians.

(*Pause.*)

And sent 'em scurryin' home. Well! That's sort o' what ya might call a typical day!

(*Bravos from everyone except the* GRAND DUKE.)

GRAND DUKE

(*Russian speech, quite angry.*)

INTERPRETER

His Excellency says he would like to kill a Comanche also.

BUFFALO BILL
Hm?

GRAND DUKE
(*With obvious jealousy.*)
Like Boofilo Beel!

INTERPRETER
Like Buffalo Bill!

GRAND DUKE
(*Excited Russian speech.*)

INTERPRETER
He will *prove* he cannot be intimidated!

GRAND DUKE
Rifle, rifle, rifle!

BUFFALO BILL
(*To* BUNTLINE.)
I think my story may've worked a bit too well.

BUNTLINE
Nonsense! This is *terrific!*
(*They duck as the* GRAND DUKE, *cackling madly, scans the surrounding darkness over his rifle sight.*)
Shows you've won the Grand Duke's heart.

GRAND DUKE
(*Pounding his chest.*)
Boofilo Beel! *I* . . . am *BOOFILO BEEL!*
(*He laughs demonically.*)

BUNTLINE
I think you'd better find 'm a Comanche.

BUFFALO BILL
Right! *Well.* Um . . .
(*Slight laugh.*)
That *could* be a . . . problem.

GRAND DUKE
Comanche! *Comanche!*

BUFFALO BILL
Ya see, fer one thing, the Comanches live in Texas. And we're in Missouri.

GRAND DUKE

COMANCHE! *COMANCHE!*

BUFFALO BILL

Fer another, I ain't 'xactly sure what they look like.

GRAND DUKE

Ah!

(*He fires into the darkness.*

SPOTTED TAIL *stumbles out, collapses and dies.*

The GRAND DUKE *and his* INTERPRETER *delirious with joy.* BUNT-LINE *dumfounded.* BUFFALO BILL *stunned, but for vastly different reasons.*)

BUNTLINE

(*Approaching the body cautiously.*)

My God, will you look at that? Fate must be smiling!

(*He laughs weakly, stares up at the heavens in awe.*

BUFFALO BILL, *almost in a trance, walks over to the body; stares down at it.*

Weird music heard.

The lights change color, grow vague.

All movement arrested.

SPOTTED TAIL *rises slowly and moves just as slowly toward the* GRAND DUKE; *stops.*)

SPOTTED TAIL

My name is Spotted Tail. My father was a Sioux; my mother, part Cherokee, part Crow. No matter how you look at it, I'm just not a Comanche.

(*He sinks back to the ground.*

Lights return to normal, the music ends.)

GRAND DUKE

(*Baffled Russian speech.*)

INTERPRETER

His Excellency would like to know what the man he just shot has said.

(*Long pause.* BUFFALO BILL *looks around, as if for help; all eyes upon him.*)

BUFFALO BILL

(*Softly.*)

He said . . .

(*Pause.*)

"I . . .

(*Pause.*)

should have . . .

(*He looks at* BUNTLINE, *takes a deep breath.*)

stayed at home in . . . Texas with the rest of my . . . Comanche tribe."

BUNTLINE

Fabulous!

(*He takes* SPOTTED TAIL's *picture; the night sky glows from the flash.*)

Absolutely fabulous!

(*The scene fades around* BUFFALO BILL, *who stands in the center, dizzily gripping his head.*

Scene 4

(*Dimly we see the* SENATORS *and* SITTING BULL's INDIANS *glide back into view.*)

BUFFALO BILL

If it *please* the honorable senators . . . there is something I would like to say to *them*, as well.

(*Pause.*)

I wish to say . . . that there is far more at stake here, today, than the discovery of Indian grievances.

(*Pause.*)

At stake are these people's lives.

(*Pause.*)

In *some* ways, more than even that. For these are not just *any* Indians. These are *Sitting Bull's* Indians. . . . The last to surrender.

(*Pause.*)

The last of a kind.

(*Long pause.*)

So, in that way, you see, they are . . . perhaps more *important* for us than . . . any others.

(*Pause.*)

For it is we, alone, who have put them on this strip of arid land. And what becomes of them is . . . our responsibility.

(BUFFALO BILL *stares helplessly as the scene about him fades to black.*)

VOICE
And now, for your *pleasure*, BUFFALO BILL'S WILD WEST
SHOW *PROUDLY* PRESENTS . . .
(*Lights to black.*
Drum roll.)

Scene 5

(*Stage dark; drum roll continues. Weirdly colored spotlights begin to crisscross on the empty stage.*)

VOICE

THE MOST FEROCIOUS INDIAN ALIVE! . . .

(*The bars of a large round cage slowly emerge from the floor of the stage; then, around the bars, the Wild West Show fence seen earlier.*)

THE FORMER SCOURGE OF THE SOUTHWEST! . . .

(*The lights on the fence begin to glow; eerie, fantastical atmosphere.*

A tunnel-cage rolls out from the wings and connects with the large central cage.

Sound of an iron grate opening offstage.

Rodeo music up.)

The one 'n only . . . *GERONIMO!*

(*Enter* GERONIMO, *crawling through the tunnel; as soon as he is in sight, he stops, lifts his head, takes in his surroundings.*

Enter two COWBOY ROUSTABOUTS *with prods. They are enormous men—much larger than life-size. Their muscles bulge against their gaudy clothes. Their faces seem frozen in a sneer. Even their gun belts are oversized.*

They prod GERONIMO *along, raise the gate to the center cage and coax him in, closing it behind him. Then they move away.*

26

GERONIMO (Ed Rombola)

GERONIMO *paces about, testing the bars with his hands.*)
GERONIMO
I AM GERONIMO! WAR CHIEF OF THE GREAT CHIRI-
CAHUA APACHES!
(*He stalks about.*)
Around my neck is a string of white men's genitals! MEN I
HAVE KILLED! . . . Around my waist, the scalplocks of
white women's genitals! WOMEN I RAPED AND KILLED!
. . . *No Indian has ever killed or raped more than I!* Even the
Great Spirits cannot count the number! . . . My body is
painted with blood! I am red from white men's BLOOD! . . .
NO ONE LIVES WHO HAS KILLED MORE WHITE MEN
THAN *I!*
(BUFFALO BILL, *in his fancy buckskin, enters unnoticed by*
GERONIMO; *drum roll. He opens the cage door and walks inside.*

Once inside, he closes the door and stands still. GERONIMO
*senses his presence and stops moving. Lifts up his head as if to
hear better. Sniffs. Turns. Stares at* BUFFALO BILL.

Slowly, BUFFALO BILL *walks toward him. He stops just short
of the Indian. Then defiantly turns his back.*

GERONIMO *practically frothing.*

Long pause. GERONIMO *does nothing.*

BUFFALO BILL *walks calmly away, opens the cage door, and
exits. Disappears into the shadows.*

GERONIMO *stands trembling with frenzy.*

Lights fade to black.)

Scene 6

(*Lights up on the Senate Committee,* SITTING BULL'S INDIANS, *and* BUFFALO BILL.)

SENATOR LOGAN

Mister Grass, I wonder if you could be a bit more *specific* and tell us *exactly* what you think the Great Father has promised which he has not given.

JOHN GRASS

He promised to give us *as much as we would need, for as long as we would need it!*

SENATOR DAWES

Where did he promise you *that?*

JOHN GRASS

In a treaty.

SENATOR LOGAN

What treaty?

JOHN GRASS

A treaty signed some years ago, maybe five or six.

SENATOR LOGAN

Mister Grass, many treaties were signed five or six years ago. But frankly, I've never heard of an arrangement quite like that one.

JOHN GRASS

You took the Black Hills from us in this treaty!

SENATOR DAWES

You mean we *bought* the Black Hills in it!

29

(LOGAN *glares at* DAWES.)

JOHN GRASS

I have nothing else to say.

(*He turns and starts to walk away.*)

SENATOR LOGAN

Mister Grass! The . . . Senator . . . *apologizes* for his . . . tone.

(*Pause.* JOHN GRASS *returns.*)

JOHN GRASS

If you *bought* the Black Hills from us, where is our money?

SENATOR LOGAN

The money is in trust.

JOHN GRASS

Trust?

SENATOR MORGAN

He means, it's in a bank. Being *held* for you in a . . . bank. In *Washington!* Very . . . fine bank.

JOHN GRASS

Well, we would rather hold it ourselves.

SENATOR DAWES

The Great Father is worried that you've not been educated enough to spend it *wisely*. When he feels you have, you will receive every last penny of it. *Plus interest.*

(JOHN GRASS *turns in fury;* LOGAN *totally exasperated with* DAWES.)

BUFFALO BILL

Mister Grass, *please!* These men have come to *help* you! But their ways are *different* from yours; you must be *patient* with them.

JOHN GRASS

You said you would bring us the Great Father.

BUFFALO BILL

I *tried!* I *told* you! But he wouldn't come; *what else could I do?*

JOHN GRASS

You told us he was your *friend.*

BUFFALO BILL

HE *IS* MY FRIEND! *Look, don't you understand?* These men are your *only hope.* If you turn away from them, it's like . . . *committing suicide.*
(*Pause.*)

JOHN GRASS
(*To the* SENATORS.)
At Fort Laramie, Fort Lyon, and Fort Rice we signed treaties, parts of which have never been fulfilled.

SENATOR DAWES
Which parts have never been fulfilled?

JOHN GRASS
At Fort Rice the Government advised us to be at *peace,* and said that *if we did so,* we would receive a span of horses, five bulls, ten chickens, and a wagon!

SENATOR LOGAN
You . . . really believe . . . these things were in the treaty?

JOHN GRASS
We were told they were.

SENATOR LOGAN
You . . . saw them written?

JOHN GRASS
We cannot read very well, but we were *told* they were!
(*The* SENATORS *glance sadly at one another.* JOHN GRASS *grows confused. Pause.*)
We were also . . . promised a STEAMBOAT!

SENATOR MORGAN
A *steamboat?*

SENATOR DAWES
What in God's name were you supposed to do with a steamboat in the middle of the plains?
(*He laughs.*)

JOHN GRASS
I don't know.
(*He turns in confusion and stares at* BUFFALO BILL; BUFFALO BILL *turns helplessly to the* SENATORS. *As——*

JOHN GRASS (Sam Waterston)

Lights begin to fade.)

SITTING BULL

Where is the Great Father, Cody? . . . The one you said would help us. . . . The one you said you knew *so well.*
(*As lights go to black, a Mozart minuet is heard.*)

Scene 7

*(Lights up on White House Ballroom, in the center of which
is a makeshift stage. The front drop of this stage is a melodramatic western-heroic poster with* "Scouts of the Plains, *by
NED BUNTLINE" painted over it.*

The Mozart stops as——

A Negro USHER *enters.)*

USHER

This way, Mister President.

OL' TIME PRESIDENT

(Offstage.)

Thank you, George.

(Enter the OL' TIME PRESIDENT *in white tie and tails, cigar in
mouth, brandy glass in hand.)*

This way, dear. They're about to start.

(Enter the FIRST LADY *in a formal gown.)*

FIRST LADY

Oh, this *is* exciting! Our *first* real cowboys!

(The USHER *leads them toward a pair of Louis XIV chairs set
facing the stage. Drum roll.)*

OL' TIME PRESIDENT

Sssh. Here we go.

(They sit.

Enter, from behind the canvas drop, NED BUNTLINE. *He wears
an exaggerated version of a plainsman's outfit.)*

NED BUNTLINE

Mister President, hon'rable First Lady,
Before you stands a character most shady,
A knave whose presence darkens this bright earth,
More than does the moon's eclipsing girth.
What's that you say, I'm rude to filth espouse,
When I'm the guest of such a clean, white house?
Fear not, there's somethin' I didn't mention:
Recently, I found redemption.
Ah, forgive me, I'm sorry, Ned Buntline's the name,
It's me who's brought Bill Cody fame.
Wrote twenty-seven books with him the hero.
Made 'm better known than Nero.
And though we sold 'em cheap, one for a dime,
The two of us was rich in no time.
As for my soul's redemption, it came thus:
I saw the nation profit more than us.
For with each one o' my excitin' stories,
Cody grew t' represent its glories.
Also helped relieve its conscience,
By showing pessimism's nonsense.
Later, when people asked t' *see* 'm,
I wrote a play for him to be in;
A scene of which we now perform for you,
As you've so graciously implored us to.

Cody, of course, impersonates himself,
As does Yours Truly.
The Crow Maiden is Italian actress
Paula Monduli.
Our evil Pawnee Chief, the great German actor
Gunther Hookman.
Our other Indians, I'm afraid,
Come from Brooklyn.
However, as a special treat tonight,
A visitor is here,
And I've added some new dialogue,
So he might appear.
Realize though, this man's come as Cody's friend,
He's not an actor.
Though of course in *my* play, who men *are*
Is the real factor.
So get set then for anything,
May the script be damned,
An' let's give Cody an' Wild Bill Hickok
A ROUSING HAND!

(*The* FIRST LADY *and the* OL' TIME PRESIDENT *applaud enthusiastically.* BUNTLINE *exits.*

The canvas drop is rolled up to reveal another canvas drop—a painted forest of the worst melodramatic order.

On stage, wooden as only the worst amateur actors can be, stand CODY *and* HICKOK, *the latter with long, glorious hair, fancy buckskin leggings, two large guns and a knife in his belt.*)

BUFFALO BILL

God pray we're in time. Those Pawnee devils will do anything.
(*Silence.*)

BUNTLINE

(*Prompting from offstage.*)
Especially . . .
(*Silence.*)

BUFFALO BILL
Think that's your line, Bill.
WILD BILL HICKOK
Oh, hell's thunder.
(*To* BUNTLINE.)
Better give it-a-me agin.
BUNTLINE
Especially . . .
HICKOK
Especially.
BUNTLINE
. . . at their . . .
HICKOK
At their.
BUFFALO BILL
(*Sotto voce.*)
. . . dreadful annual . . .
HICKOK
Dreadful. Annual.
BUNTLINE
. . . Festival of the Moon.
HICKOK
Festival of the Moon. Which is . . . 'bout t' happen. As it does
every . . .
(*Silence.*)
BUFFALO BILL
. . . year.
HICKOK
Year.
BUNTLINE
Very good.
HICKOK
Very good.
BUNTLINE
No!

BUFFALO BILL (Stacy Keach) and WILD BILL HICKOK (Barton Heyman)

HICKOK

Whose line's that?

BUFFALO BILL

No one's. He was jus' congratulatin' you.

HICKOK

Oh, Will, fer pity's sake, le' me out o' this.

BUNTLINE

Ad lib!

BUFFALO BILL

Yes! Pray God we're in time to stop the Pawnee's dreadful Festival of the Moon so that I, the great Buffalo Bill, can once again——

HICKOK

Will, stop it! A man may need money, but no man needs it this bad.

(*Enter* BUNTLINE, *tap-dancing the sound of horse's hooves.*)

BUFFALO BILL

Hark! Ned Buntline approaches! One o' the finest sharpshooters o' the West!

HICKOK

(*Under his breath.*)

Couldn't hit a cow in the ass from two paces.

BUFFALO BILL

Who knows? Maybe *he* can help us in our dire strait.

HICKOK

Mister and Missus President, if you're still out there, believe me, I'm as plumb embarrassed by this dude-written sissyshit as you.

BUNTLINE

HAIL, BUFFALO BILL! Hail—uh—Wild Bill Hickok. What brings you to this unlikely place?

HICKOK

Good fuckin' question.

BUNTLINE

Could it be that you seek, as I do, the camp of Uncas, evil Pawnee chief?

39

BUFFALO BILL

Yes, verily. We seek his camp so that I, the great Buffalo Bill, can, once again, save someone in distress.

(HICKOK *groans.*)

This time, specifically, a virgin maiden——

HICKOK

You gotta be jokin'.

BUFFALO BILL

Will you shut up! Named Teskanjavila! Who, 'less I save her, faces torture, sacrifice, and certain violations.

BUNTLINE

This bein' so, *let us join forces!*

HICKOK

Boy, where's your *self-respect?*

BUNTLINE

(*Weakly.*)

And save this virgin together.

BUFFALO BILL

(*To* HICKOK.)

Will you leave me alone!

HICKOK

This ain't a *proper place* for a man t' be!

BUFFALO BILL

Well, I THINK IT *IS!* I think I'm doin' a lot o' good up here! Entertainin' people! Makin' 'em *happy!* Showin' 'em the West! Givin' 'em somethin' t' be *proud* of! *You* go spend your life in Dodge City if you want! I got *bigger* things in mind!

(*Stunned pause.*)

BUNTLINE

(*Very sheepishly.*)

To repeat: let us join forces and save this virgin together.

HICKOK

Buntline, if these guns were loaded, I'd——

BUNTLINE

(*Cueing the actors offstage.*)

HARK! The maiden's name is called!

NUMEROUS VOICES
(*Offstage.*)
Teskanjavila!

BUNTLINE
We must be near the camp of Uncas.

BUFFALO BILL
Evil Pawnee chief.

HICKOK
I'm gettin' sick.

BUNTLINE
Let us, therefore, approach with caution.

BUFFALO BILL
Guns ready.

BUNTLINE
Ears open.

BUFFALO BILL
(*To* HICKOK.)
Mouths shut!

BUNTLINE
Eyes alert.

BUFFALO BILL
So that I, Buffalo Bill, may once aga——
(HICKOK *has walked over and is staring into his face.*)
Just *what are you doin'?*

HICKOK
What're *you* doin'?

BUFFALO BILL
I'm doin' what I'm doin', *that's* what I'm doin'!

HICKOK
(*To* BUNTLINE.)
Always was intelligent.

BUFFALO BILL
I am doin' what my country *wants!* WHAT MY BELOVED
COUNTRY *WANTS!*

HICKOK
(*To the First Family.*)
This . . . is . . . what you want?

FIRST LADY
Absolutely!

OL' TIME PRESIDENT
Best play I've seen in years!

(HICKOK, *staggered, sits down on the stage.*)

BUFFALO BILL
When a man has a talent, a *God*-given talent, I think it's his godly duty t' make the most of it.

(*Applause from the First Family.* BUFFALO BILL *nods acknowledgment. To* HICKOK.)

Ya see, Bill, what you fail to understand is that I'm not being false to what I *was*. I'm simply *drawin'* on what I was . . . and raisin' it to a higher level.

(*He takes a conscious pause.*)

Now. On with the show!

(*He points to* BUNTLINE, *cueing him to give the next line.*)

BUNTLINE
AVAST, AHOY! Above yon trees see the pale moon rising!

(*A cardboard moon is pulled upwards.*)

Feel the black night envelop us like a dark dream.

(BUNTLINE *and* CODY *shiver.*)

Sounds of the savage forest are heard. . . . We approach on tiptoes.

BUFFALO BILL
(*To the First Family.*)

God pray we're in time.

(*They drop to their bellies as the canvas drop is raised to reveal the camp of* UNCAS. *Tied to a totem pole is* TESKANJAVILA, *writhing sensually.*

Clearly phony INDIANS *dance around her to the beat of drums. The heroes crawl slowly forward.* HICKOK, *eyeing the girl lustfully, joins in.*)

FIRST LADY
That Hickok's rather handsome, isn't he?

OL' TIME PRESIDENT
I'm watching the girl. Note her legs. How white they are. For an Indian. One can almost see the soft inner flesh of her thighs.

FIRST LADY

This play excites me!

OL' TIME PRESIDENT

We really should have more things like this at the White House. (*The drums grow wilder. The* INDIANS *scream;* BUNTLINE, CODY, *and* HICKOK *invade the Indian camp site. Gunshots.* INDIANS *fall dead.*)

TESKANJAVILA

(*Italian accent.*)

Saved! A maiden's prayers are answered! And may I say, not a bit too soon! Already, my soft thighs had been pried open; my budding breasts pricked by the hot tip of an Indian spear. Yet, through it all, my maidenhead stayed secure. Here. In this pouch. Kept in this secret pocket. Where no one thought to look. Thus is innocence preserved! May Nazuma, God of Thunder, grant me happiness!

(*Thunder heard.*)

HICKOK

Buntline write that speech?

BUFFALO BILL

I think she changed it a little.

(UNCAS *rises from the dead.*)

UNCAS

(*German accent.*)

I am Uncas, Chief of the Pawnee Indians, recently killed for my lustful ways. Yet, before the white men came and did me in, I had this vision: the white man is great, the red man nothing. So, if a white man kills a red man, we must forgive him, for God intended man to be as great as possible, and by eliminating the inferior, the great man carries on God's work. Thus, the Indian is in no way wronged by being murdered. Indeed, quite the opposite: being murdered is his purpose in life. This was my recent vision. Which has brought light to the darkness of my otherwise useless soul. . . . And now, I die again.

(*He collapses.*)

HICKOK

Buntline write that?

43

BUFFALO BILL

Think Hookman changed it also. They all do it. It's our style. I dunno, people seem to like it.

HICKOK

Yeah? Well then, guess it mus' be my turn!

(*He pulls out his bowie knife.*)

BUFFALO BILL

HEY!

HICKOK

Make one false move an' I'll rip you 'part, friend or no.

BUNTLINE

Bill, look——

HICKOK

As for you, Buntline, you fangless lizard, you harmless bull, you ball of——

BUNTLINE

BRING DOWN THE CURTAIN!

HICKOK

First one touches that curtain, I cuts int' mincemeat an' eats fer dinner, *raw!*

FIRST LADY

I'm trembling all over.

HICKOK

Okay, Buntline. Now we're gonna settle up the score.

BUNTLINE

Score?

HICKOK

Men jus' don' humiliate Wil' Bill Hickok.

BUNTLINE

Hu—humiliate?

HICKOK

Or leastways don' do it twice, bein' dead shortly after the first occasion.

BUNTLINE

Wh—what . . . 're you talkin' about?

HICKOK

'Bout havin' to impersonate myself. 'Bout the humiliation o' havin' to impersonate my *own personal self!*

BUNTLINE

Oh.

FIRST LADY

Fantastic!

BUNTLINE

Well, I dunno what t' say.

HICKOK

It weren't in the deal!

BUNTLINE

Deal?

HICKOK

You said if I came here, I could play Bat Masterson!

BUNTLINE

Ah, *that!*

(*He chuckles.*)

Well, . . . if you recall, I said *maybe* you could play Bat Masterson. First, we had t' see how good you did as Hickok.

HICKOK

As *Hickok?* Chrissake, I AM Hickok!

BUNTLINE

Right.

HICKOK

Well, why in hell should I play *him* then?

BUNTLINE

Well, there's audience appeal.

FIRST LADY

There sure is!

BUNTLINE

BILL! Now—now, wait-a-second! Let's talk this over. Like gentlemen.

BUFFALO BILL

Yeah. Right. Let's . . . not get too . . . carried away. After all——

HICKOK

If you don' stay out o' this, I'm gonna slit yer stuffin' gizzard an' extract, inch by inch, what's guts in most folks, but in you is thorou' garbage.

BUFFALO BILL

Now wait-a-minute! Hold on! You—you think I'm jus' gonna stand here an'——

HICKOK

Oh, shut up! Dumb, dudelickin' FRAUD!

BUFFALO BILL

What?

HICKOK

If I gotta play Hickok, I'm gonna play Hickok the way Hickok should be *played!*

BUNTLINE

Put that knife away, please! . . . For godsakes. Cody, *HELP ME! Cody!*

(BUNTLINE *falls, a knife in his back. He crawls off the front of the stage; collapses.*)

FIRST LADY

He looks kind o' dead.

(BUFFALO BILL *heads for the body, stunned.*)

HICKOK

Sorry, Will. Guess I just ain't used to show business yet.

(*He chuckles and turns his attention to* TESKANJAVILA. BUFFALO BILL *is feeling for* BUNTLINE'S *pulse.*)

TESKANJAVILA

O, *Sancta Maria,* I don' like this gleam in his eye.

HICKOK

(*Striking a pose.*)

> Hail, sweet cookie, tart of tempting flavors,
> Why've I been denied your spicy favors?

TESKANJAVILA

AH! *What're you doing?* HELP!

(HICKOK *unties her from the pole, at the same time unhooking his gun belt. He works rapidly.*

BUFFALO BILL *lets* BUNTLINE'*s limp arm drop. He stares back at the stage, stunned.*)

FIRST LADY

Ooooh, look what he's doing now!

(*The First Family climb on the stage, the Negro* USHERS *bringing their chairs for them so they can have a more comfortable view.*)

Really, we must invite this theatre crowd more often.

(HICKOK *is now standing above* TESKANJAVILA, *who lies helpless at his feet.* BUFFALO BILL *watches from offstage, outside the ring. Also helpless.*)

HICKOK

Hickok, fastest shooter in the West, 'cept for Billy the Kid, who ain't as accurate; Hickok, deadliest shooter in the West, 'cept for Doc Holliday, who wields a sawed-off shotgun, which ain't fair; Hickok, shootinest shooter in the West, 'cept for Jesse James, who's absolutely indiscriminate; this Hickok, strong as an eagle, tall as a mountain, swift as the wind, fierce as a rattlesnake—a legend in his own time, or any other—this Hickok stands now above an Indian maiden——

TESKANJAVILA

I'm not an Indian and I'm not a maiden!

HICKOK

Who's not an Indian and not a maiden, but looks pretty good anyhow—an' asks those o' you watchin' t' note carefully the basic goodness of his very generous intentions, since otherwise . . .

(*He starts to finger her clothing.*)

. . . they might be mistaken for . . .

(*He rips open her buckskin dress.*)

. . . *LUST!*

(*She is left in a frilly Merry Widow corset.*)

TESKANJAVILA

Eh, bambino. If you don' mind, I'd like a little privacy.

(*To the First Family.*)

After all, I've not rehearsed this.

(HICKOK *pulls the cord, lowering the curtain.*)

47

OL' TIME PRESIDENT
Good show, Cody! *Good show!*

(BUFFALO BILL, *in a daze, walks to the stage and opens the curtain.*

"Scouts of the Plains" *drop seen. He stares at it. Pulls it down.*
NO ONE THERE.

Mozart minuet heard.

He looks around in total confusion.

The stage and all the White House furniture begin to disappear.

Lights fade to black, BUFFALO BILL *spinning dizzily in the middle.*

Music fades.)

Scene 8

(*Lights up again on the Senate Committee.*)

SENATOR LOGAN

Mister Grass. Let's leave aside the question of the steamboat. You mentioned the treaty at Fort Lyon and said that parts of that treaty had never been fulfilled. Well, I happen to be quite familiar with that particular treaty and happen to know that it is the Indians who did not fulfill its terms, not us.

JOHN GRASS

We did not *want* the cows you sent!

SENATOR LOGAN

You signed the treaty.

JOHN GRASS

We did not understand that we were to give up part of our reservation in exchange for these cows.

SENATOR DAWES

Why'd you think we were giving you twenty-five thousand cows?

JOHN GRASS

We were hungry. We thought it was for food.

SENATOR LOGAN

It wasn't explained that *only* if you gave us part of your reservation would you receive these cows?

JOHN GRASS

Yes. That was explained.

SENATOR MORGAN

And yet, you thought it was a gift.

JOHN GRASS

Yes.

SENATOR LOGAN

In other words, you thought you could have both the cows and the land?

JOHN GRASS

Yes.

SENATOR DAWES

Even though it was explained that you couldn't.

JOHN GRASS

Yes.

SENATOR MORGAN

This is quite hard to follow.

SENATOR LOGAN

Mister Grass, tell me, which would you prefer, cows or land?

JOHN GRASS

We prefer them both.

SENATOR LOGAN

Well, what if you can't have them both?

JOHN GRASS

We prefer the land.

SENATOR LOGAN

Well then, if you knew you had to give up some land to get these cows, why did you sign the treaty?

JOHN GRASS

The white men made our heads dizzy, and the signing was an accident.

SENATOR LOGAN

An accident?

JOHN GRASS

They talked in a threatening way, and whenever we asked questions, shouted and said we were stupid. Suddenly, the Indians around me rushed up and signed the paper. They were like men stumbling in the dark. I could not catch them.

SENATOR LOGAN

But you signed it, too.

(*Long pause.*)

SENATOR DAWES

Mister Grass. Tell me. Do the Indians really expect to keep all this land and yet do nothing toward supporting themselves?

JOHN GRASS

We do not have to support ourselves. The Great Father promised to give us everything we ever needed; for that, we gave him the Black Hills.

SENATOR LOGAN

Mister Grass. Which do you prefer—to be self-sufficient or to be given things?

JOHN GRASS

We prefer them both.

SENATOR DAWES

Well, you can't *have* them both!

BUFFALO BILL

Please!

JOHN GRASS

I only know what we were promised.

SENATOR DAWES

That's *not* what you were promised!

JOHN GRASS

We believe it is.

BUFFALO BILL

What's going on here?

SENATOR MORGAN

Mister Grass. Wouldn't you and your people like to live like the white man?

JOHN GRASS

We are happy like the Indian!

SENATOR LOGAN

He means, you wouldn't like to see your people made *greater,* let's say?

JOHN GRASS

That is not possible! The Cheyenne and the Sioux are as great as people can be, already.

SENATOR MORGAN

Extraordinary, really.

BUFFALO BILL

Mister Grass. Surely . . . *surely* . . . your people would like to *improve their condition!*

JOHN GRASS

We would like what is owed us! If the white men want to give us more, that is fine also.

SENATOR LOGAN

Well, we'll see what we can do.

SENATOR MORGAN

Let's call the next. This is getting us nowhere.

JOHN GRASS

We would especially like the money the Great Father says he is holding for us!

SENATOR DAWES

I'm afraid that may be difficult, since, in the past, we've found that when an Indian's been given money, he's spent it all on liquor.

JOHN GRASS

When he's been given money, it's been so little there's been little else he could buy.

SENATOR MORGAN

Whatever, the Great Father does not like his Indian children getting drunk!

JOHN GRASS

Then tell the Great Father, who says he wishes us to live like white men, that when an Indian gets drunk, he is merely imitating the white men he's observed!

(*Laughter from the* INDIANS. LOGAN *raps his gavel.*)

SENATOR DAWES

STOP IT!

(*No effect.* LOGAN *raps more.*)
What in God's name do they think we're doing here? STOP IT!
(*Over the* INDIANS' *noise, the noise of a Wild West Show is heard; lights fade to black.*)

Scene 9

(*Wild West Show music and crisscrossing multicolored spot-lights. The rodeo ring rises from the stage, its lights glittering. Wild West Show banners descend above the ring.*)

VOICE

And now, ladies and gentlemen, let's hear it for Buffalo Bill's fantastic company of authentic western heroes . . . the fabulous ROUGHRIDERS OF THE WORLD!

(*Enter, on heroically artificial horses, the* ROUGHRIDERS—*themselves heroically oversized.*

They gallop about the ring in majestic, intricate formation, whoopin' and shootin' as they do.)

With the ever-lovely . . . ANNIE OAKLEY!

(ANNIE OAKLEY *performs some startling trick shots as the others ride in circles about her.*)

And now, once again, here he is—the star of our show, the Ol' Scout himself; I mean the indestructible and ever-popular——

(*Drum roll.*)

——BUFFALO BILL!

(*Enter, on horseback,* BUFFALO BILL. *He is in his Wild West finery.*

He tours the ring in triumph while his ROUGHRIDERS *ride after him, finally exiting to leave him in the center, alone.*)

BUFFALO BILL

THANK YOU, THANK YOU! A *GREAT* show lined up to-night! With all-time favorite Johnny Baker, Texas Jack and his twelve-string guitar, the Dancin' Cavanaughs, Sheriff Brad and the Deadwood Mail Coach, Harry Philamee's Trained Prairie Dogs, the Abilene County Girls' School Trick Roping and Lasso Society, Pecos Pete and the——

VOICE

Bill.

BUFFALO BILL

(*Startled.*)

Hm?

VOICE

Bring on the Indians.

BUFFALO BILL

What?

VOICE

The *Indians.*

BUFFALO BILL

Ah.

(BUFFALO BILL *looks uneasily toward the wings as his company of* INDIANS *enters solemnly and in ceremonial warpaint; they carry the Sun Dance pole. At its summit is a buffalo skull.*)

And now, while my fabulous company of authentic . . . American Indians go through the ceremonial preparations of the Sun Dance, which they will re-create in all its death-defying goriness—let's give a warm welcome back to a courageous warrior, the magnificent Chief Joseph——

(*Some* COWBOY ROUSTABOUTS *set up an inverted tub; music for* CHIEF JOSEPH'S *entrance.*)

——who will recite his . . . celebrated speech. CHIEF JOSEPH!

(*Enter* CHIEF JOSEPH, *old and hardly able to walk.*)

CHIEF JOSEPH

In the moon of the cherries blossoming, in the year of our surrender, I, Chief Joseph, and what remained of my people, the Nez Percés, were sent to a prison in Oklahoma, though General Howard had promised we could return to Idaho, where we'd always lived. In the moon of the leaves falling, still in the year

of our surrender, William Cody came to see me. He was a nice man. With eyes that seemed . . . frightened; I . . . don't know why. He told me I was courageous and said he admired me. Then he explained all about his Wild West Show, in which the great Sitting Bull appeared, and said if I agreed to join, he would have me released from prison, and see that my people received food. I asked what I could do, as I was not a very good rider or marksman. And he looked away and said, "Just repeat, twice a day, three times on Sundays, what you said that afternoon when our army caught you at the Canadian border, where you'd been heading, and where you and your people would have all been safe." So I agreed. For the benefit of my people. . . . And for the next year, twice a day, three times on Sundays, said this to those sitting around me in the dark, where I could not see them, a light shining so brightly in my eyes!
(*Pause.*

He climbs up on the tub.

Accompanied by exaggerated and inappropriate gestures.)
"Tell General Howard I know his heart. I am tired of fighting. Our chiefs have been killed. Looking Glass is dead. The old men are all dead. It is cold and we have no blankets. The children are freezing. My people, some of them, have fled to the hills and have no food or warm clothing. No one knows where they are—perhaps frozen. I want to have time to look for my children and see how many of them I can find. Maybe I shall find them among the dead. Hear me, my chiefs. I am tired. My heart is sick and sad. From where the sun now stands, I will fight no more forever. . . . "
(*He climbs down from the tub.*)
After which, the audience always applauded me.
(*Exit* CHIEF JOSEPH. *Pause.*)

    BUFFALO BILL

The Sun Dance . . . was the one religious ceremony common to all the tribes of the plains. The Sioux, the Crow, the Black-

CHIEF JOSEPH (George Mitchell)

An Absolutely Original and Heroi

The Only One which Kings, Chief Rulers, Famous Generals, Nobles and the Most Illustrious and Enlightened Men of Every
Theme of Artistic, Poetic and Historic Inspiration. Which of All the Millions it has Entertained, Taught and Transporte

COL. CODY'S ONLY CARD

TO THE PUBLIC.

"Wild West and
Congress of Rough Riders
of the World"

W. F. CODY
"BUFFALO BILL"

If Any Seek to Imitate It, They Defraud	It Controls All the Genuine Material of Its Kind
If Any Claim to Rival It, They Falsify	It Alone Commands the Confidence of Potentates & Powers
If Any Copy Its Announcements, It Is Forgery	It Is the Only Exhibition With Which Governments Co-operate

THE ONLY EXHIBITION IN ALL THE WORLD THAT HAS

READ THESE MEMORABLE WORDS O

"BILLY; FOR MY CHILDREN AND GRANDCHILDREN, WHO CAN

LADIES AND GENTLEMEN: PERMIT ME TO
INTRODUCE TO YOU
A CONGRESS OF ROUGH
RIDERS
OF THE
WORLD.

BUFFALO WILD BILL'S WE

CONGRESS OF ROUGH RIDERS OF THE WORL

OF ITS KIND THE FIRST, THE ONLY, AND THE LAST, IT IS A REVELATION

THE MOST COLOSSAL AND THE STRANGEST ENTERTAINMENT EVER ORGANIZED OR DREAMED OF.

The Only Object Teacher History has Ever Had, or Recreation Furnished.	Promoted by Kings, Honored by Nations. A Paragon at Home, a Triumph Abroad.
Whatever Others May Say or Claim, the Whole World Pronounces it Supremely and Originally Great.	Rough Riders Schooled to Hardship, and to Whom the Saddle is an Heirloom.
The Mirror of American Manhood. The Camp of the Makers of a Nation's History.	An Equine and Equestrian Study, with Horse and Man a Sculptor's Beau Ideal.

Hazardous Pastimes of which the Great Plains and Deserts are the Natural Playground.

A HOLIDAY REFLECTING YEARS OF ROMANCE

AND THE REALITY OF IMPERISHABLE DEEDS.

FEATS OF FEARLESS SKILL, FASHIONED BY NECESSITY,

PERFECTED IN DANGER, AND CROWNED BY VICTORY.

THE ONE PRESENTMENT OF GRIM-VISAGED WAR BEFORE THE STARTLED FACE OF SMILING PEACE.

MAKING THE NEW WORLD AND THE OLD APPEAR IN

BRAVEST AND MOST BRILLIANT RIVALRIES

ITSELF A NOBLE PART OF WHAT IT SHOWS, WHICH OFTEN SEEN THE MORE ATTRACTIVE GROWS.

ic Enterprise of Inimitable Lustre.

NATE SALSBURY, Vice-President.

To America and Americans

After months of industrious prepara-
tion, continous outlay and most diligent
and thorough inquiry, in presenting this
greatly enlarged and perfected exhibition
to the approval of my countrymen for
the season of 1893, I beg to direct their
special consideration to the fact.

That it is an absolutely original crea-
tion, without precedent, or parallel, and
which can have no successor.

That it is just as genuine as original,
in every presentation and as regards
every participant.

That its Scouts, Cowboys, Indians and
Horsemen, were a part of the seasoned
history which it, and it alone, personi-
fies, forever and regards it living lessons
of heroic prowess, arms and pastimes.

That its representative and extraordinary riders, horsemen and others are
of the nationalities stated and the dis-
tinction claimed.

That it will steadfastly continue to
deserve the world-wide fame and recog-
nition previously and gloriously won,
now and forever, as far above deception
as it is beyond rivalry or imitation.

Very respectfully,
NATE SALSBURY,

More Than Historic; It Is History Itself in Living Lessons	NOT AN EMPTY CHEATING ECHO, BUT DARING DEEDS INCARNATE
Not the Imitations of Fancy, but the Stupendous Realism of Facts	TELLING ITS THRILLING TALES WITH RIFLE, SWORD and SPEAR
Not a Speculation of Apes, but an Institution of Heroes	USING IN PLACE OF HALTING WORDS INSPIRING, SPLENDID, ACTION

NO COUNTERPART. EXCLUSIVELY ITS OWN CREATION.

GENERAL SHERMAN TO COL. CODY:

"NEVER SEE THESE THINGS AS WE SAW THEM, I THANK YOU."

ITS GREAT ORIGINATOR NOW RIDES ALONE UPON FAME'S WARPATH
THE LAST IN SERVICE OF THE GREATER SCOUTS TO WHOM OUR ARMY'S SAFETY WAS ENTRUSTED.

The Master Horseman, More Picturesque and Perfect than Alexander on Bucephalus.
Commanding the Grand Host of All the World's Most Noted Riders.
No Toppling Tents Could Cover Such An Equestrian Gathering of Nations.

No Hundred Theatres Combined Inclose its Proud Reviews and Battle Spectacles.
The Plains, the Steppes, the Pampas, Are its Platform.
The Free Range of the Open Air, the Coliseum Nature Builds for It.

Among Its Features, Martial Pageants, Dazzling Reviews, Savage Displays of Fearful War and Foray.

Wild & Most Wondrous Riders on Naked Steeds
STRANGE AND EXCITING NOMADIC RACES.

THE REGULAR CAVALRY OF MANY FLAGS.   DESERT-BORN BEDOUINS IN AMAZING FEATS

THE THRILLING EPISODES, STRUGGLES, ESCAPES, ADVENTURES, MARKSMANSHIP AND UNIQUE PASTIMES OF BORDER LIFE.

REGULAR ARTILLERY JUST AS IN ACTION
THE WARLIKE ACTS AND ARMS OF MANY LANDS.

NOT ONE OF WHICH CAN EVER ELSEWHERE BE PRODUCED OR DUPLICATED

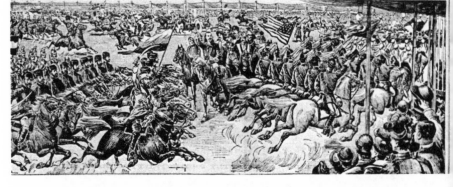

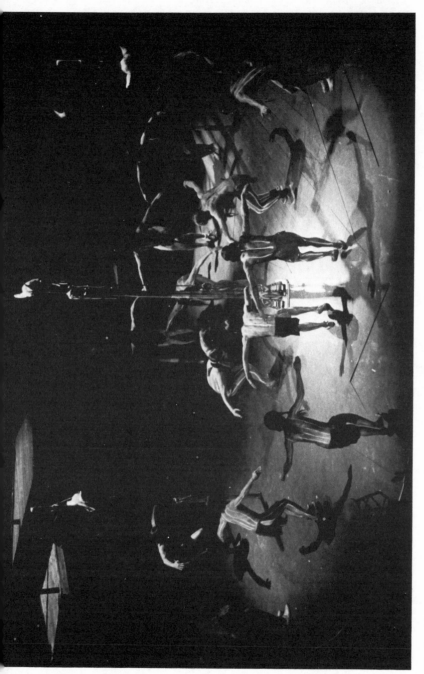

The Sun Dance

feet, the Kiowa, the Blood, the Cree, the Chippewa, the Arap-
aho, the Pawnee, the Cheyenne. It was *their* way of proving
they were . . . real Indians.
(*Pause.*)
The bravest would take the ends of long leather thongs and
hook them through their chest muscles, then, pull till they'd
ripped them out. The greater the pain they could endure, the
greater they felt the Spirits would favor them. Give them what
they needed. . . . Grant them . . . salvation.
(*Pause.*)
Since the Government has officially outlawed this ritual, we
will merely imitate it.
(*Pause.*)
And no one . . . will be hurt.
(*He steps back.*

The dance begins. The INDIANS *take the barbed ends of long
leather thongs that dangle from the top of the Sun Dance
pole and hook them through plainly visible chest harnesses.
Then they pull back against the center and dance about it,
flailing their arms and moaning as if in great pain.*

Suddenly JOHN GRASS *enters.* A ROUSTABOUT *tries to stop him.*

The INDIANS *are astonished to see this intruder;* BUFFALO BILL
stunned.

JOHN GRASS *pulls the* INDIANS *out of their harnesses, rips open
his shirt, and sticks the barbs through his chest muscles.*

He chants and dances. The other INDIANS, *realizing what he's
doing, blow on reed whistles, urge him on. Finally he collapses,
blood pouring from his chest.*

The INDIANS *gather around him in awe.*

BUFFALO BILL *walks slowly toward* JOHN GRASS; *stares down at
him.*

The INDIANS *remove the Sun Dance pole and trappings.*

BUFFALO BILL *crouches and cradles* JOHN GRASS *in his arms.*

As lights fade to black.)

Scene 10

(*Light up on* WHITE HOUSE USHER.)

USHER

The President is exercising in the gym, sir. This way.

(*Enter* BUFFALO BILL.)

BUFFALO BILL

You're sure it's all right?

USHER

Yes, sir. He said to show you right in. Very pleased you're here.
(*The* USHER *gestures for* CODY *to pass. When he does, the* USHER *bows, turns, and leaves.*

BUFFALO BILL *stops.*

Gym noise heard.

Lights up on the OL' TIME PRESIDENT, *dressed like* HICKOK *and astride a mechanical horse pushed by another* USHER. *Near him sits an old Victrola;* "On the Old Chisholm Trail" *is playing.*

The OL' TIME PRESIDENT *spurs his horse onwards.*

Nearby hangs a punching bag.

BUFFALO BILL *stares at the scene, stupefied; walks cautiously forward.*)

BUFFALO BILL

Uh——

OL' TIME PRESIDENT

Cody! My ol' buddy! Welcome back! Long time no see!

62

BUFFALO BILL

Yes, sir. Long time . . . no see.

OL' TIME PRESIDENT

Wha'd'ya think o' this thing? Latest in athletic equipment. Just got it yesterday.

BUFFALO BILL

It's a . . . nice imitation.

OL' TIME PRESIDENT

More power.

USHER

Pardon?

OL' TIME PRESIDENT

Little more power.

(*The* USHER *nods; the mechanical horse bounces faster.*)

Good for the figure, this bronco riding. GIDDYAP! You orn'ry sonofabitch.

(*He laughs; whips his horse furiously.*)

BUFFALO BILL

Sir. What I've come t' talk t' you about is very important.

OL' TIME PRESIDENT

Can't hear ya. Speak up!

BUFFALO BILL

(*Pointing to the phonograph.*)

May I turn this down?

OL' TIME PRESIDENT

Tell me. You think I look a little bit like Hickok?

BUFFALO BILL

Mr. President, would you *please stop this?*

OL' TIME PRESIDENT

What?

BUFFALO BILL

STOP THIS!!!

OL' TIME PRESIDENT

Whoa, Nellie.

USHER

Pardon?

63

OL' TIME PRESIDENT
WHOA, NELLIE!
(*The* USHER *stops the horse; shuts off the phonograph.*
Cold tone.)
All right. What is it?

BUFFALO BILL
Well sir, I'm here t' ask if you'd come with me t' Sitting Bull's
reservation.

OL' TIME PRESIDENT
Whose reservation?

BUFFALO BILL
Sitting Bull's. He was in my Wild West Show for a time. And
naturally, I feel a sort o' . . . obligation.
(*Pause.*)
Personal . . . obligation.

OL' TIME PRESIDENT
I see.

BUFFALO BILL
I figure you're just about the only one left now who can really
help him. His people are in a desperate way.

OL' TIME PRESIDENT
Tell me: this—uh—Sitting Bull. Isn't he the one who wiped out
Custer?

BUFFALO BILL
Uh, well, yes, he . . . is, but it was, ya know, nothin'—uh—
personal.
(*Weak laugh.*)

OL' TIME PRESIDENT
Can't help.

BUFFALO BILL
What?

OL' TIME PRESIDENT
I'm sorry, but I can't help.

BUFFALO BILL
You don't understand the *situation!*

OL' TIME PRESIDENT

I *don't?* All right, let's say I *want* to help. *What do I do for*
'em? Do I give 'em back their land? Do I resurrect the buffalo?

BUFFALO BILL

You can do *other* things!

OL' TIME PRESIDENT

No, Cody. *Other* people can do other things. *I* . . . must do
magic. Well, I can't *do* magic for *them;* it's too late.

BUFFALO BILL

I promised Sitting Bull you'd come.

OL' TIME PRESIDENT

Then you're a fool.

BUFFALO BILL

They're going to *die.*

(*Long pause.*)

OL' TIME PRESIDENT

Tell ya what. 'Cause I'm so *grateful* to you. . . . For your Wild
West Show. For what it's *done.* For this country's *pride,* its
glory.

(*Pause.*)

I'll do you a favor; I'll send a committee in my place.

BUFFALO BILL

A committee *won't be able to help!*

OL' TIME PRESIDENT

Oh, I think the gesture will mean something.

BUFFALO BILL

To WHOM?

(*Silence.*)

OL' TIME PRESIDENT

Being a great President, Cody, is like being a great eagle. A
great . . . *hunted* eagle. I mean, you've got to know . . .
when t' stay put.

(*He smiles.*)

On your way out, Bill, tell the guards, no more visitors today,
hm?

(He nods to the USHER, *who starts to rock him again.*
As BUFFALO BILL *slowly leaves.*
Music back up.
Lights fade to black.)

Scene 11

(*Lights up on reservation, as when last seen.*

The INDIANS *are laughing; the* SENATORS, *rapping for silence.*)

SENATOR DAWES

What in God's name do they think we're doing here?

BUFFALO BILL

(*To* SITTING BULL.)

Please! You must tell them to stop this *noise!*

SITTING BULL

You told us you would bring the Great Father.

BUFFALO BILL

I told you! He couldn't come! It's not my fault! Besides, these men are the Great Father's representatives! Talking to them is like talking to him!

SITTING BULL

If the Great Father wants us to believe he is wise, why does he send us men who are *stupid?*

BUFFALO BILL

They're *not* stupid! They just don't see things the way *you* do!

SITTING BULL

Yes. Because they are stupid.

BUFFALO BILL

They're *not stupid!*

SITTING BULL

Then they must be blind. It is the only other explanation.

BUFFALO BILL

All right. Tell me. Do *you* understand them?

SITTING BULL

Why should I want to understand men who are stupid?

BUFFALO BILL

Because if you *don't,* your people will *starve to death.*
(*Long pause.*)
All right. . . . Now. Let me try to explain some . . . *basics.*
(*To the* SENATORS.)
Well, as you've just seen, the Indian can be hard t' figure.
What's one thing t' us is another t' him. For example, farmin'.
Now the *real* problem here is not poor soil. The real problem's
plowin'. Ya see, the Indian believes the earth is sacred and sees
plowin' as a sacrilegious act. Well, if ya can't get 'em t' plow,
how can ya teach 'em farmin'? Impossible. Fertile land's another problem. There just ain't much of it, an' what there is, the
Indians prefer to use for pony racin'. Naturally, it's been explained to 'em how people can race ponies anywhere, but they
prefer the fertile land. They say, if their ancestors raced ponies
there, that's where *they* must race. . . . Another difficult problem is land itself. The majority of 'em, ya see, don't understand
how land can be owned, since they believe the land was made
by the Great Spirits for the benefit of everyone. So, when we do
buy land from 'em, they think it's just some kind o' temporary
loan, an' figure we're kind o' foolish fer payin' good money for
it, much as someone 'ud seem downright foolish t' us who paid
money fer the sky, say, or the ocean. Which . . . causes
problems.
(*Pause.*)
Well, what I'm gettin' at is *this:* if *their* way o' seein' is hard
fer *us* t' follow, ours is just as hard fer *them.* . . . There's an
old Indian legend that when the first white man arrived, he
asked some Indians for enough land t' put his blanket down
onto fer the night. So they said yes. An' next thing they knew,
he'd unraveled this blanket till it was one long piece o' thread.
Then he laid out the thread, an' when he was done, he'd roped

BUFFALO BILL (Stacy Keach) and SITTING BULL (Manu Tupou)

off a couple o' square miles. Well, the Indian finds that sort o' behavior hard t' understand. That's all I have t' say. Maybe, if you think about it, some good'll finally come from all this. I dunno.

SENATOR MORGAN

Thank you. We *shall* think about it. And hope the Indians think about it, too. And cause no more disturbances like the one just now. . . . Ask Sitting Bull if he has anything to say.

BUFFALO BILL

Sitting Bull.

SITTING BULL

Of course I will speak if they desire me to. I suppose it is only such men as they desire who may say anything.

SENATOR LOGAN

Anyone here may speak. If you have something to say, we will listen. Otherwise, sit down.

SITTING BULL

Tell me, do you know who I am, that you talk as you do?

BUFFALO BILL

SITTING BULL, PLEASE!

(*Long pause.*)

SITTING BULL

I wish to say that I fear I spoke hastily just now. In calling you . . . stupid. For my friend William Cody tells me you are here with good intentions. So I ask forgiveness for my unthinking words, which might have caused you to wreak vengeance on my people for what was not their doing, but *mine, alone.*

SENATOR LOGAN

We are pleased you speak so . . . sensibly. You are . . . forgiven.

SITTING BULL

I shall tell you, then, what I want you to say to the Great Father for me. And I shall tell you everything that is in my heart. For I know the Great Spirits are looking down on me today and want me to tell you everything that is in my heart. For you are the only people now who can help us.

(*Pause.*)

My children . . . are dying. They have no warm clothes, and their food is gone. The old way is gone. No longer can they follow the buffalo and live where they wish. I have prayed to the Great Spirits to send us back the buffalo, but I have not yet seen any buffalo returning. So I know the old way is gone. I think . . . my children must learn a *new* way if they are to live. Therefore, tell the Great Father that if he wishes us to live like white men, we will do so.

(*Stunned reaction from his Indians. He silences them with a wave of his hand.*)

For I know that if that pleases him, we will benefit. I am looking always to the benefit of my children, and so, want only to please the Great Father. . . . Therefore, tell him for me that I have never yet seen a white man starving, so he should send us food so we can live like the white man, as he wants. Tell him, also, we'd like some healthy cattle to butcher—I wish to kill three hundred head at a time. For that is the way the white man lives, and we want to please the Great Father and live the same way. Also, ask him to send us each six teams of mules, because that is the way the white men make a living, and I want my children to make as good a living. I ask for these things only because I was advised to follow your ways. I do not ask for anything that is not needed. Therefore, tell him to send to each person here a horse and buggy. And four yokes of oxen and a wagon to haul wood in, since I have never yet seen a white man dragging wood by hand. Also, hogs, male and female, and male and female sheep for my children to raise from. If I leave anything out in the way of animals that the white men have, it is a mistake, for I want every one of them! For we are great Indians, and therefore should be no less great as white men. . . . Furthermore, tell him to send us warm clothing. And glass for the windows. And toilets. And clean water. And beds, and blankets, and pillows. And fur coats, and gloves. And hats. And *pretty silk ties*. As you see, I do not ask for anything that is not needed. For the Great Father has advised us to live like

71

white men, so clearly, this is how we should live. For it is your
doing that we are here on this reservation, and it is not right
for us to live in poverty. And be treated like beasts. . . . That
is all I have to say.

SENATOR LOGAN

I want to say something to that man before he sits down, and
I want all the Indians to listen very carefully to what I'm going
to tell him. . . . Sitting Bull, this committee invited you to
come here for a friendly talk. When you talked, however, you
insulted them. I understand this is not the first time you have
been guilty of such an offense.

SITTING BULL

Do you know who I am that you talk the way you do?

SENATOR LOGAN

I know you are Sitting Bull.

SITTING BULL

Do you really not recognize me? Do you really not know who
I am?

SENATOR LOGAN

I said, I know you are Sitting Bull!

SITTING BULL

You know I am Sitting Bull. But do you know what *position*
I hold?

SENATOR DAWES

We do not recognize any difference between you and other
Indians.

SITTING BULL

Then I will tell you the difference. So you will never ever make
this mistake again. I am here by the will of the Great Spirits,
and by their will I am a chief. My heart is red and sweet, and
I know it is sweet, for whatever I pass near tries to touch me
with its tongue, as the bear tastes honey and the green leaves
lick the sky. If the Great Spirits have chosen anyone to be
leader of their country, know that it is not the Great Father;
it is myself.

SENATOR DAWES

WHO IS THIS CREATURE?

SITTING BULL

I will show you.

(*He raises his hand. The* INDIANS *turn and start to leave.*)

SENATOR LOGAN

Just a minute, Sitting Bull!

(SITTING BULL *stops.*)

Let's get something straight. You said to this committee that you were chief of all the people of this country and that you were appointed chief by the Great Spirits. Well, I want to say that you were *not* appointed by the Great Spirits. Appointments are not made that way. Furthermore, I want to say that you are arrogant and stupidly proud, for you are not a great chief of this country or any other; that you have no following, no power, no control, and no right to any control.

SITTING BULL

I wish to say a word about my not being a chief, having no authority, being proud——

SENATOR LOGAN

You are on an Indian reservation merely at the sufferance of the Government. You are fed by the Government, clothed by the Government; your children are educated by the Government, and all you have and are today is because of the Government. I merely say these things to notify you that you cannot insult the people of the United States of America or its committees. And I want to say to the rest of you that you must learn that you are the equals of other men and must not let this one man lead you astray. You must stand up to him and not permit him to insult people who have come all this way just to help you. . . . That is all I have to say.

SITTING BULL

I wish to say a word about my not being a chief, having no authority, being proud, and considering myself a great man in general.

SENATOR LOGAN

We do not care to talk with you any more today.

SENATOR DAWES

Next Indian.

SITTING BULL

I said, I wish to speak about my having no authority, being not a chief, and——

SENATOR LOGAN

I said, we've heard enough of you today!

(SITTING BULL *raises his hand; the* INDIANS *leave.*

SITTING BULL *stares at* CODY.)

SITTING BULL

If a man is the chief of a great people, and has lived only for those people, and has done many great things for them, *of course he should be proud!*

(*He exits.*

Lights fade to black.)

Scene 12

(*Guitar heard:* "Chisholm Trail."

Lights up on saloon. Most of it is in shadows. Only a poker table is well lit.

A bar is in the distance.

Swinging doors.

Various COWBOYS *slouch about.*)

JESSE JAMES

(*Sings.*)

> Walkin' down the street in ol" Dodge City,
> Wherever I look things look pretty shitty.
>> Coma ti yi youpy, youpy yea, youpy yea,
>> Coma ti yi youpy, youpy yea.
> An' the very worst thing that I can see,
> Is a dead man walkin' straight toward me.
>> Coma ti yi youpy, youpy yea, youpy yea,
>> Coma ti yi youpy, youpy yea.
> This dead man clearly ain't feelin' well,
> If you ask me I think he's just found hell.
>> Coma ti yi youpy, youpy yea, youpy yea,
>> Coma ti yi youpy, you——

(*Enter* BUFFALO BILL *in an overcoat flecked with snow. Gloves. A warm scarf.*)

BUFFALO BILL

Where's Hickok? I'm told Hickok's here. . . . *Where's Hickok?*

BILLY THE KID

Hey, uh . . . stranger.

(*He chuckles.*

Before he can draw, BUFFALO BILL *gets the drop on him.*)

BUFFALO BILL

Who're you?

PONCHO

He . . . is the original . . . Billy the Kid.

(JESSE JAMES *makes a move and* BUFFALO BILL *draws his other gun; gets the drop on him as well.*)

And *he* is the original Jesse James. The original Doc Holliday is, I'm afraid, out to lunch.

(*The* COWBOYS *move to encircle* BUFFALO BILL.)

Who're *you?*

BUFFALO BILL

Buffalo Bill.

PONCHO

Really?

(PONCHO *laughs. Enter* HICKOK.)

HICKOK

Cody! My ol' buddy!

(*They embrace.*)

Oh, great balls o' fire! What a surprise! Why jus' this mornin' I was . . . was . . .

(*Pause.*)

picturin' you.

BUFFALO BILL

You were?

HICKOK

So how ya been? C'mon. Tell me.

BUFFALO BILL

Oh, I been . . . fine.

HICKOK

Great!

BUFFALO BILL

An' you?

HICKOK

Never better. *Never better!*

BUFFALO BILL

Mus' say, you've sure got some . . . famous . . . people here.
(*Slight laugh.*)

HICKOK

Well, ya know, it's . . . that kind o' place.
(*He laughs, too; slaps* CODY *on the back. He leads him to a
table.*)
So! . . . Whatcha doin' here? Great honor. *Great honor!*

BUFFALO BILL

I hafta . . . *talk* . . . t' you.

HICKOK

Sure thing.
(*He waves the* COWBOYS *away; they sit at the table in privacy.*)

BUFFALO BILL

I've just come from Sitting Bull's reservation.

HICKOK

Oh?
(*Slight laugh.*)
That reservation's a far piece from here.

BUFFALO BILL

I need your help! Sitting Bull is . . .
(*Pause.*)

HICKOK

What?
(*Long silence.*)

BUFFALO BILL

I'm scared. . . . I dunno what's happenin' anymore. . . .
Things have gotten . . . *beyond* me.
(*He takes a drink.*)
I see them *everywhere.*
(*Weak smile; almost a laugh.*

Music.

INDIANS *appear in the shadows beyond the saloon.*)

BUFFALO BILL (Stacy Keach) and WILD BILL HICKOK (Barton Heyman)

In the grass. The rocks. The branches of dead trees.
(*Pause.*)
Took a drink from a river yesterday an' they were even there,
beneath the water, their hands reachin' up, I dunno whether
beggin', or t' . . . drag me under.
(*Pause.*)
I wiped out their food, ya see. . . . Didn't *mean* to, o' course.
(*He laughs to himself.*)
I mean IT WASN'T MY FAULT! The railroad men needed
food. They *hired* me t' *find* 'em food! Well. How was *I* t' know
the goddam buffalo reproduced so slowly? *How was I to know
that?* NO ONE KNEW THAT!
(*Pause.*

The INDIANS *slowly disappear.*)
Now, Sitting Bull is . . .
(*Long pause.*)

HICKOK
What?

BUFFALO BILL
The . . . hearing was a shambles. I brought these Senators,
you see. To Sitting Bull's reservation. It . . . was a shambles.
(*Pause.*)
So we left. He . . . *insulted* them.
(*Pause.*)
Then I saw the letter.
(*Silence.*)

HICKOK
What letter?

BUFFALO BILL
The letter to McLaughlin. The letter ordering . . . it to be
. . . done.
(*Pause.*)
So I rode back. Rode all night. Figuring, maybe . . . if I can
just *warn* him. . . . But the reservation soldiers stopped me
and . . . made me . . . drink with them. And by the time I
got there, he . . . was dead. The greatest Indian who'd ever

79

lived. Shot. By order of the Government. Shot with a Gatling gun.
(*Pause.*)
While the . . . wonderful, gray horse I'd given him for . . . appearing in my show danced his repertory of tricks in the background. Since a gunshot was his cue to perform.
(*He laughs.*
Stops.
Long silence.)

HICKOK

Well now. In exactly what way did you imagine *I* could . . . *help* this . . . situation?

BUFFALO BILL

You have what I *need* . . . now.

HICKOK

(*Smiling slightly.*)
Oh?

BUFFALO BILL

I'm *scared,* you see.
(*Pause.*)
Scared . . . not . . . so much of *dyin',* but . . . dyin' *wrong.*
(*Slight laugh.*)
Dyin' . . . in the center of my arena with . . . makeup on.
(*Long pause.*)
Then I thought of you. . . . Remembered that night in the White House. Remembered thinking, "My God! Look at Hickok. Hickok *knows just who he is!*"
(*Pause.*)
"Hickok has the answer," I said. . . . Hickok knows who he *is.*
(*Pause.*)
I must see Hickok again.
(*Long silence.*)

HICKOK

Well I'm glad you came. Yes. Glad . . . to be able to . . . help.
(*Pause.*)

Funny. That night, in the White House, I remember thinking: "My God, it's *Cody* who's got the answer!"

BUFFALO BILL

. . . What?

HICKOK

Poncho!

PONCHO

Si, señor.

HICKOK

Bring in our . . . um . . .

PONCHO

Ah! *Si, señor! Ahorita.*

(*Exit* PONCHO.)

HICKOK

Naturally, at first, you may be a bit startled. Put off. Not . . . exactly . . . what you *had in mind.* Yet! I'm sure that once you *think* about it, you'll agree *it's the only way.* Just like Jesse has. Billy. Doc Holliday. The boys.

BUFFALO BILL

What are you talkin' about?

HICKOK

Why, takin' what you were and raisin' it to a . . . higher level. (*He laughs.*)

Naturally, for my services, I get a small fee. Percentage. You get 50 per cent right off the top. Of course, if at any time you aren't happy, you can leave. Take your business elsewhere. That's written in. Keeps us on our toes. Mind you, this . . . *enterprise* . . . is still in its infancy. The *potential,* though . . . is unlimited. For example, think of this. The *great national good* . . . that could come from this: some of you, let's say, would concentrate strictly on theatrics. MEANWHILE! *Others* of you would concentrate on purely humanitarian affairs. Save . . . well, not Sitting Bull, but . . . some Indian down in Florida. Another up in Michigan. Perhaps expand into Canada. Mexico. Central America. SOUTH AMERICA! My God, there must be literally *millions* of people who could benefit by your presence! Your . . . *simultaneous presence!*

PONCHO

Here they are, *señor!*

(*Enter a group of men dressed as* BUFFALO BILL. *Their faces are covered by masks of his face. They wear his florid buckskin clothes—if anything, even more elaborately designed.*)

HICKOK

Naturally, we've still got a few wrinkles to iron out. Color of hair. Color of eyes. That sort of thing. But with *you* here, exercising artistic control, why, we could go on like this *forever!*

(BUFFALO BILL, *stunned by the sight, fires his guns at the duplicate Codys. They fall and immediately rise again.*

They slowly surround him.

He screams as he shoots.

They disappear.

The saloon fades to black.

BUFFALO BILL *alone on stage.*)

BUFFALO BILL

AND NOW TO CLOSE! AND *NOW TO CLOSE!*

VOICE

Not *yet.*

(*Pause.*)

They also killed the rest of his tribe.

(*Music.*

INDIANS *enter mournfully. They carry a large white sheet.*

Sound of wind.

BUFFALO BILL *watches, then moves slowly away; exits.*)

Scene 13

(*The* INDIANS *cover the center area with the huge white sheet, then lie down upon it in piles.*

Enter COLONEL FORSYTH, *a* LIEUTENANT, *and two* REPORTERS, *their coat collars turned up for the wind.* CODY *is with them; he carries a satchel.*)

FIRST REPORTER

Fine time of year you men picked for this thing.

COLONEL FORSYTH

They're heathens; they don't celebrate Christmas.

FIRST REPORTER

I don't mean the date, I mean the weather.

COLONEL

Uncomfortable?

FIRST REPORTER

Aren't you?

COLONEL

One gets used to it.

SECOND REPORTER

Colonel, I gather we lost twenty-nine men, thirty-three wounded. How many Indians were killed?

COLONEL

We wiped them out.

SECOND REPORTER

Yes, I know. But how many *is* that?

COLONEL

We haven't counted.

LIEUTENANT

The snow has made it difficult. It started falling right after the battle. The bodies were covered almost at once. By night they were frozen.

COLONEL

We more than made up for Custer, though, I can tell you that.

SECOND REPORTER

But Custer was killed fifteen years ago!

COLONEL

So what?

LIEUTENANT

If there are no more questions, we'll take you to——

FIRST REPORTER

I have one! Colonel Forsyth, some people are referring to your victory yesterday as a massacre. How do you feel about that?

COLONEL

One can always find someone who'll call an overwhelming victory a massacre. I suppose they'd prefer it if we'd let more of our own boys get shot!

FIRST REPORTER

Then you don't think the step you took was harsh?

COLONEL

Of course it was harsh. And I don't like it any more than you. But had we shirked our responsibility, skirmishes would have gone on for years, costing our country millions, as well as untold lives. Of course innocent people have been killed. In war they always are. And of course our hearts go out to the innocent victims of this. But war is not a game. It's tough. And demands tough decisions. In the long run I believe what happened here at this reservation yesterday will be justified.

FIRST REPORTER

Are you implying that the Indian Wars are finally over?

COLONEL

Yes, I believe they're finally over. This ludicrous buffalo religion of Sitting Bull's people was their last straw.

SECOND REPORTER

And now?

COLONEL

The difficult job of rehabilitating begins. But that's more up General Howard's line.

LIEUTENANT

Why don't we go and talk with him? He's in the temporary barracks.

COLONEL

He can tell you about our future plans.

(*They start to leave.*)

BUFFALO BILL

You said you'd——

LIEUTENANT

Ah, yes, it's that one.

(*He points to a body.*)

BUFFALO BILL

Thank you.

(*He stays. The others leave; he stares at the grave.* SITTING BULL *has entered, unnoticed.* BUFFALO BILL *takes a sprig of pine from the satchel and is about to put it on the grave.*)

SITTING BULL

Wrong grave. I'm over here. . . . As you see, the dead can be buried, but not so easily gotten rid of.

BUFFALO BILL

Why didn't you listen to me? I *warned* you what would happen! Why didn't you *listen?*

(*Long silence.*)

SITTING BULL

We had land. . . . You wanted it; you took it. That . . . I understand perfectly. What I cannot understand . . . is why you did all this, *and at the same time* . . . professed your love.

(*Pause.*)

SITTING BULL (Manu Tupou)

BUFFALO BILL

Well . . . well, what . . . about *your* mistakes? *Hm?* For, for example: you were very unrealistic . . . about things. For . . . example: did you *really* believe the buffalo would return? *Magically* return?

SITTING BULL

It seemed no less likely than Christ's returning, and a great deal more useful. Though when I think of their reception here, I can't see why either would really want to come back.

BUFFALO BILL

Oh, God. Imagine. For awhile, I actually thought my Wild West Show would *help.* I could give you money. Food. Clothing. And also make people *understand* things . . . better.
(*He laughs to himself.*)
That was my reasoning. Or, anyway, *part . . .*
(*Pause.*)
of my reasoning.

SITTING BULL

(*Slight smile.*)
Your show was very popular.
(*Pause.*)

BUFFALO BILL

We had . . . *fun,* though, you and I.
(*Pause.*)
Didn't we?

SITTING BULL

Oh, yes. And that's the terrible thing. We had all surrendered. We were on reservations. We could not fight, or hunt. We could do nothing. Then you came and allowed us to imitate our glory. . . . It was humiliating! For sometimes, we could almost imagine it was *real.*

BUFFALO BILL

Guess it wasn't so authentic, was it?
(*He laughs slightly to himself.*)

SITTING BULL

How could it have been? You'd have killed all your performers in one afternoon.

(Pause.)

BUFFALO BILL

You know what worried me most? . . . The fear that I might die, in the middle of the arena, with all my . . . makeup on. *That* . . . is what . . . worried me most.

SITTING BULL

What worried *me* most . . . was something I'd said the year before. Without thinking.

BUFFALO BILL

(Softly.)

What?

SITTING BULL

I'd agreed to go onto the reservation. I was standing in front of my tribe, the soldiers leading us into the fort. And as we walked, I turned to my son, who was beside me. "Now," I said, "you will never know what it is to be an Indian, for you will never again have a gun or pony. . . ." Only later did I *realize* what I'd said. These things, the gun and the pony—they came with you. And then I thought, ah, how terrible it would be if we finally owe to the white man not only our destruction, but also our glory. . . . Farewell, Cody. You were my friend. And, indeed, you still are. . . . I never killed you . . . because I *knew it would not matter.*

(He starts to leave.)

BUFFALO BILL

If only I could have saved *your* life!

(SITTING BULL stops and stares at him coldly; turns and leaves. Long pause.)

BUFFALO BILL

Well! This is it!

(He forces a weak laugh.)

Naturally, I've been thinking 'bout this moment for quite some time now. As any performer would.

VOICE

And now to close!

BUFFALO BILL

NOT YET! . . . I would . . . first . . . like to . . . say a few
words in defense of my country's Indian policy, which seems, in
certain circles, to be meeting with considerable disapproval.
(*He smiles weakly, clears his throat, reaches into his pocket,
draws out some notes, and puts on a pair of eyeglasses.*)
The—uh—State of Georgia, anxious to solidify its boundaries
and acquire certain valuable mineral rights, hitherto held ac-
cidentally by the Cherokee Indians, and anxious, furthermore,
to end the seemingly inevitable hostilities between its residents
and these Indians on the question of land ownership, initiated,
last year, the forced removal of the Cherokee nation, resettling
them in a lovely and relatively unsettled area west of the
Mississippi, known as the Mojave Desert. Given proper irriga-
tion, this spacious place should soon be blooming. Reports that
the Cherokees were unhappy at their removal are decidedly
untrue. And though many, naturally, died while marching from
Georgia to the Mojave Desert, the ones who did, I'm told, were
rather ill already, and nothing short of medication could have
saved them. Indeed, in all ways, our vast country is speedily
being opened for settlement. The shipment of smallpox-
infested blankets, sent by the Red Cross to the Mandan Indians, has, I'm pleased to say, worked wonders, and the
Mandans are no more. Also, the Government policy of exter-
minating the buffalo, a policy with which I myself was in-
timately connected, has practically reached fruition. Almost no
buffalo are now left, and soon the Indians will be hungry
enough to begin farming in earnest, a step we believe necessary if they are ever to leave their barbaric ways and enter
civilization. Indeed, it is for this very reason that we have
begun giving rifles to the Indians as part of each treaty with
them, for without armaments they could not hope to wage
war with us, and the process of civilizing them would be
seriously hampered in every way. Another aspect of our
benevolent attitude toward these savages is shown by the
Government's policy of having its official interpreters translate

everything incorrectly when interpreting for the Indians, thereby angering the Indians and forcing them to learn English for themselves. Which, of course, is the first step in civilizing people. I'm reminded here of a story told me by a munitions manufacturer. It seems, by *accident,* he sent a shipment of blank bullets to the Kickapoo Indians, and . . .
(*He looks around.*)
Well, I won't tell it. It's too involved. I would just like to say that I am sick and tired of these sentimental humanitarians who take no account of the difficulties under which this Government has labored in its efforts to deal fairly with the Indian, nor of the countless lives we have lost and atrocities endured at their savage hands. I quote General Sheridan:——
(*The* INDIANS *have begun to rise from their graves; for a while they stand in silence behind* BUFFALO BILL, *where they are joined, at intervals, by the rest of the* INDIAN *company.*)
——"I do not know how far these so-called humanitarians should be excused on account of their political ignorance; but surely it is the only excuse that can give a shadow of justification for their aiding and abetting such horrid crimes as the Indians have perpetrated on our people."

BUFFALO BILL
The excuse that the Indian way of life is vastly different from ours, and that what seem like atrocities to us do not to them, does not hold water, I'm afraid!

For the truth is, the Indian never had any real title to the soil of this country. We had that title. By *right of discovery!* And all the Indians were, were the *temporary occupants* of the

SITTING BULL
(*Very softly.*)
I am Sitting Bull——

(*Almost inaudible.*)
——and I am—
dying!

BLACK HAWK
Black Hawk *is dying.*

TECUMSEH
Tecumseh *is dying.*

land. They *had* to be
vanquished by us! It was,
in fact, our *moral obligation!*

For the earth was given to
mankind to support the
greatest number of which it
is capable; and no tribe or
people have a *right* to
withhold from the wants
of others! For example——

——in the case of Lone Wolf
versus Hitchcock, 1902, the
Supreme Court of the United
States ruled that the power
exists to abrogate the pro-
visions of *any* Indian treaty
if the *interests of the country
demand!*

Here's another one: in the
case of the Seneca Indians
versus the Pennsylvania
Power Authority, the courts
ruled that the Seneca Treaty
was invalid since perpetuity
was legally a vague phrase.
Vague phrase! Yes. Ah.
Here's one, even better.
In the——

No. Wait. Got it. The one
I've been looking for. In
the case of Sitting Bull

CRAZY HORSE
Crazy Horse . . . is dying.

RED CLOUD
Red Cloud *is dying.*

SPOTTED TAIL
Spotted Tail . . . is dying
again.

SATANTA
Satanta *is dying.*

KIOKUK
Kiokuk *is dying.*

GERONIMO
Geronimo . . . *is dying!*

OLD TAZA
Old Taza *is dying!*

JOHN GRASS
John Grass is dying.

(*Long pause.*)

(*The* INDIANS *begin a soft and
mournful moaning.*)

91

versus Buffalo Bill, the
Supreme Court ruled that the
inadvertent slaughter of . . .
buffalo by . . . I'm sorry,
I'm . . . reminded here of an
amusing story told me by
General Custer. You
remember him—one o' the
great dumbass . . .

(*Pause.*)

BUFFALO BILL

Think I'd better close. I . . . just want to say that anyone who thinks we have done something wrong is *wrong!* And that I have here, in this bag, some——

(*He goes and picks up his satchel; he looks up and sees the* INDIANS *staring at him; he turns quickly away.*)

——Indian trinkets. Some . . . examples of their excellent workmanship. Moccasins. Beads. Feathered headdresses for your children.

(*He has begun to unpack these trinkets and place them, for display, on a small camp stool he has set across the front edge of the center ring.*)

Pretty picture postcards. Tiny Navaho dolls. The money from the sale of these few trifling trinkets will go to help them help themselves. Encourage them a bit. You know, *raise their spirits.* . . . Ah! Wait. No, sorry, that's a—uh—buffalo skin.

(*He shoves it back in the satchel.*)

Yes. Here it is! Look, just look . . . at this handsome replica of an . . . Indian. Made of genuine wood.

(*He puts the carved head of an Indian on the camp stool so that it overlooks all the other trinkets.*

The lights now slowly begin to fade on him; he sits by the trinkets, trembling.)

CHIEF JOSEPH

Tell General Howard I know his heart. I am tired of fighting. Our chiefs have been killed. Looking Glass is dead. The old

BUFFALO BILL (Stacy Keach)

men are all dead. It is cold and we have no blankets. The children are freezing. My people, some of them, have fled to the hills and have no food or warm clothing. No one knows where they are—perhaps frozen. I want to have time to look for my children and see how many of them I can find. Maybe I shall find them among the dead.

(*Almost all the lights are now gone;* CHIEF JOSEPH *can hardly be seen;* BUFFALO BILL *is but a shadow. Only the trinkets are clear in a pinspot of light, and that light, too, is fading.*)

Hear me, my chiefs. I am tired. My heart is sick and sad. From where the sun now stands, I will fight no more, forever.

(*And then, very slowly, even the light on the trinkets fades. And the stage is completely dark.*

Then, suddenly, all lights blazing!

Rodeo ring up.

Rodeo music.

Enter, on horseback, the ROUGHRIDERS OF THE WORLD. *They tour the ring triumphantly, then form a line to greet* BUFFALO BILL, *who enters on his white stallion. He tours the ring, a glassy smile on his face.*

The ROUGHRIDERS *exit.*

BUFFALO BILL *alone, on his horse. He waves his big Stetson to the unseen crowd.*

Then, INDIANS *appear from the shadows outside the ring; they approach him slowly.*

Lights fade to black.

Pause.

Lights return to the way they were at the top of the show, when the audience was entering.

The three glass cases are back in place.

No curtain.)

DRAMABOOKS
(Plays)

WHEN ORDERING, please use the Standard Book Number consisting of the publisher's prefix, 8090–, plus the five digits following each title. (Note that the numbers given in this list are for paperback editions only. Many of the books are also available in cloth.)

Elmer Rice: Three Plays (Adding Machine, Street Scene, Dream Girl) (0735–5)
The Day the Whores Came Out to Play Tennis . . . by Arthur Kopit (0736–3)
Platonov by Anton Chekhov (0737–1)
Ugo Betti: Three Plays (The Inquiry, Goat Island, The Gambler) (0738–X)
Jean Anouilh Vol. 3 (Thieves' Carnival, Medea, Cécile, Traveler Without Luggage,
   Orchestra, Episode in the Life of an Author, Catch As Catch Can) (0739–8)
Max Frisch: Three Plays (Don Juan, The Great Rage of Philip Hotz, When the War
   Was Over) (0740–1)
New American Plays Vol. 2 ed. by William M. Hoffman (0741–X)
Plays from Black Africa ed. by Fredric M. Litto (0742–8)
Anton Chekhov: Four Plays (The Seagull, Uncle Vanya, The Cherry Orchard, The
   Three Sisters) (0743–6)
The Silver Foxes Are Dead and Other Plays by Jakov Lind (The Silver Foxes Are Dead,
   Anna Laub, Hunger, Fear) (0744–4)
New American Plays Vol. 3 ed. by William M. Hoffman (0745–2)
The Modern Spanish Stage: Four Plays, ed. by Marion Holt (The Concert at Saint Ovide,
   Condemned Squad, The Blindfold, The Boat Without a Fisherman) (0746–0)
Life Is a Dream by Calderón (0747–9)
New American Plays Vol. 4 ed. by William M. Hoffman (0748–7)

THE NEW MERMAIDS
Bussy D'Ambois by George Chapman (1101–8)
The Broken Heart by John Ford (1102–6)
The Duchess of Malfi by John Webster (1103–4)
Doctor Faustus by Christopher Marlowe (1104–2)
The Alchemist by Ben Jonson (1105–0)
The Jew of Malta by Christopher Marlowe (1106–9)
The Revenger's Tragedy by Cyril Tourneur (1107–7)
A Game at Chess by Thomas Middleton (1108–5)
Every Man in His Humour by Ben Jonson (1109–3)
The White Devil by John Webster (1110–7)
Edward the Second by Christopher Marlowe (1111–5)
The Malcontent by John Marston (1112–3)
'Tis Pity She's a Whore by John Ford (1113–1)
Sejanus His Fall by Ben Jonson (1114–X)
Volpone by Ben Jonson (1115–8)
Women Beware Women by Thomas Middleton (1116–6)
Love for Love by William Congreve (1117–4)
The Spanish Tragedy by Thomas Kyd (1118–2)

SPOTLIGHT DRAMABOOKS
The Last Days of Lincoln by Mark Van Doren (1201–4)
Oh Dad, Poor Dad . . . by Arthur Kopit (1202–2)
The Chinese Wall by Max Frisch (1203–0)
Billy Budd by Louis O. Coxe and Robert Chapman (1204–9)
The Firebugs by Max Frisch (1206–5)
Andorra by Max Frisch (1207–3)
Balm in Gilead and Other Plays by Lanford Wilson (1208–1)
Matty and the Moron and Madonna by Herbert Lieberman (1209–X)
The Brig by Kenneth H. Brown (1210–3)
The Cavern by Jean Anouilh (1211–1)
Saved by Edward Bond (1212–X)
Eh? by Henry Livings (1213–8)
The Rimers of Eldritch and Other Plays by Lanford Wilson (1214–6)
In the Matter of J. Robert Oppenheimer by Heinar Kipphardt (1215–4)
Ergo by Jakov Lind (1216–2)
Biography: A Game by Max Frisch (1217–0)
Indians by Arthur Kopit (1218–9)
Narrow Road to the Deep North by Edward Bond (1219–7)
Ornifle by Jean Anouilh (1220–0)
Inquest by Donald Freed (1221–9)
Lemon Sky by Lanford Wilson (1222–7)
The Night Thoreau Spent in Jail by Jerome Laurence and Robert E. Lee (1223–5)

For a complete list of books of criticism and history of the drama, please write to
Hill and Wang, 72 Fifth Avenue, New York, New York 10011.

DRAMABOOKS
(History and Criticism)

WHEN ORDERING, please use the Standard Book Number consisting of the publisher's prefix, 8090-, plus the five digits following each title. (Note that the numbers given in this list are for paperback editions only. Many of the books are also available in cloth.)

For a complete list of plays (including the New Mermaids and Spotlight Dramabooks series), please write to Hill and Wang, 72 Fifth Avenue, New York, New York 10011.

LITTLE COUNTRY THEATRE